9132 VICTOR!

Three got into a plane,

Only I walked away

9132 VICTOR!

Three got into a plane,

Only I walked away

JENNIFER TRUMAN

Table of Contents

Dedication

I dedicate this book to the memory of my mother and father.
They were not only my parents, they were my best friends.
You are gone, but not forgotten.
I will always love you.
William "Bill" H.M. Truman
Diana "Dani" Truman

August 09, 1942 – August 21, 2004
December 08, 1943 – August 22, 2004

~~~~

Jennifer Truman * 9132 victor!

Jennifer Truman * 9132 victor!

Additional Dedication

This book is dedicated to Darlene Roy. You began as a neighbor and quickly became a best friend. While I was living at the hospital you were my secretary. I cannot thank you enough for everything you have done for me. Everyone should be so lucky to have a neighbor and friend like you.

Thank you.

Additional Acknowledgement

Thank you Fred and Denise

Thank you to Ken Hopf for being the ATC on the other end. It may not have been the outcome everyone hoped for, but at least we know.

Thank you to Donna Duncan for many years of Wednesday lunches.

PROLOGUE

THE CITIZEN NEWSPAPER
"EMERGENCY LANDING"

Local woman talked down by controller.

Aug 9, 2004, Gilford – A 30-year-old local woman with little piloting experience managed to land her parents' small plane at Laconia Airport Monday afternoon after her father, the plane's pilot, and her mother, a passenger, passed out shortly after takeoff.

With the help of an air traffic controller, Jennifer Truman, who is from the Gilford area, landed a single-engine Piper Malibu just after 4p.m. despite having only a basic knowledge of how to fly a plane, according to Gilford Fire and Rescue officers. "It was definitely all of her hard work that avoided a potentially serious situation," said Gilford Fire Deputy Jim Hayes.

Authorities did not release the names of Truman's parents, who rescue personnel said were unresponsive upon

Jennifer Truman * 9132 victor!

*their arrival. However, the plane's tail number of N9132V
indicates the aircraft is registered to Diana L. Truman.*

*Officials at Dartmouth Hitchcock Medical Center in
Lebanon confirmed that they were treating both Dani and
William Truman both of whom were involved in an aircraft
incident earlier in the day. The couple is listed as living at 24
Pine Needle Land at Bald Peak Colony Club in Moultonboro.*

*Hayes was among several emergency personnel who
responded to the airport prepared to handle a crash.
Authorities say Boston Consolidated Terminal Radar Approach
Control (TARCON) air traffic controllers contracted rescue
crews upon receiving a report that the pilot of a plane had
become incapacitated.*

*The mother aged 60, and father in his 60's and their
daughter who was said to between 20 and 30 years old, were
the sole occupants of the six seater plane, officials said.*

*Gilford Fire Chief Mike Mooney said the plane took off
from Laconia airport and was headed for Utica, N.Y. when
trouble arose.*

Jennifer Truman * 9132 victor!

They got up into the air and a few minutes out the daughter noticed her father nodding out," said Mooney. The chief said the man eventually lost consciousness along with his wife, leaving the daughter the only one capable of landing the plane. While authorities would not disclose what caused their condition, they were said to be unresponsive when rescue crews arrived. The aircraft was reportedly full of fuel and five minutes away when the incident occurred.

Hayes said Gilford and Laconia fire departments responded to the runway with five fire rescue vehicles and two ambulances. Local fire department crews had already been at the airport earlier in the day as part of a program aimed at improving their capabilities of responding to such calls.

Rescue crews were waiting at the airport when the woman successfully set the plane down on the runway with the help of an unidentified air traffic controller. Those who witnessed the landing said Truman performed well in bringing in the craft without incident.

"She did a good job landing the plane…it bounced a few times, "said Mooney.

Jennifer Truman * 9132 victor!

Gena Adams, a pilot/instructor with Sky Bright Inc., has provided a few lessons to the younger Truman, but said the woman does not have a pilot's license. "The plane came in a little high and a little hot, but she landed it. The airplane is in one piece and they are all in one piece…that's all that counts," said Adams.

Adams said it would be easy for an inexperienced pilot to "nose" the plane directly into the runway upon landing. Airport Manager Diane Cooper said the plane did not appear to be damaged at all in the incident.

"She really put it down very nicely," said Cooper. Hayes said the incident only solidified the importance of his department having a good response plan in place for such incidents [1]

~~~~~

[1] Cunningham, Geoff, "Emergency Landing," THE CITIZEN, Page A1, A10, Tuesday, August 10, 2004

FROM MY PERSPECTIVE

~~~

February, 2009

No matter how many times I read that article, the grief, despair, terror, and disbelief still come flooding back simultaneously from that day. August 9, 2004, three people got into an airplane headed to Utica, New York. Minutes later, only one walked away from it all, and that person was me. Since that tragic day, people have speculated what happened while we were airborne. I've waited until now to break my silence and tell the truth about that horrible day. Time moves forward and I must too. I'm hoping that this book will help me to do just that; move forward. Because, sometimes I feel that I have been motionless since my parents' deaths.

As you might imagine, it has taken me awhile to write this. My family and I share the value of keeping our privacy intact. We've never been one to make brash announcements of accomplishments nor did we have an interest in keeping up with the Jones's. We lived comfortably and enjoyed a quiet lifestyle with our friends and family.

While all this was being played out on TV and in newspapers, I was at my parents sides each and every day. I didn't feel it was necessary to present myself to the media at that time. I also don't think I could have possibly have written a book at that time. My first responsibility was to my parents. Since then I have jotted down notes of the incident and memories of times with my parents. It's been 5 years but I miss my parents as much today as I did then. I say again and again, I am lucky that Mom and Dad were two of my best friends.

Each year when August 9th presents itself, I whisper a silent *"Happy Birthday, Dad"* to myself. It's the first thought I had when my alarm went off this morning in 2004. But, how do you say, *"Happy Birthday"* on such a terrible day? The sky was perfect blue, the temperature was just right but the day was sad. And, I have had a story to tell ever since.

WHEN DANI MET BILL

~~~

Chapter One

In order for me to tell the story of my parents, I feel that you should know about Bill and Dani, as people. These brief snapshots in time will hopefully provide you with a sense of who they were and why I loved them so much.

During the 60's while teenagers and young adults were making news by frolicking on a farm in upstate New York; my parents were meeting each other in college and building a life together. A decidedly more innocent and sweeter time of the era was happening just miles away.

Dani and Bill met at St. Lawrence College which seemed very fitting beginning of the life they would lead. The school was nestled in the middle of the Adirondacks of New York which offered serenity as well as a superb education. I think this story that I am about to tell reveals the playfulness and genuine affection that Dani and Bill had for each other.

Jennifer Truman * 9132 victor!

During her years at St. Lawrence, Mom became involved in a sorority. My Dad was in a fraternity. As a fundraiser, Dad's fraternity decided to have a "Slave auction." Essentially, the highest bidder for a 'slave' would have that special someone carry their books from class to class, or walk them to the library and so on. My Mom's sorority began to scout the eligible 'slaves' for her to bid on. One glance across the room proved to be the slave that the girls had been eyeing for my Mom and that was my Dad!

The auction was about to begin so my Mom rifled through her purse and eagerly pulled out her money. My mother bid with the finesse of a professional at Christie's as her sorority sisters cheered her on. The only problem was that a previous girlfriend of Dad's was also bidding as fast and furious as my mother.

A hush came over the crowd as each girl bid against the other until finally, one girl bid a dollar amount and waited for the other to counter. My mother was panicked as she was out of money. She looked desperately to her sorority sisters for help.

That one pleading look said it all as her sisters began throwing her money to outbid the girlfriend!

When the dust settled, the last girl standing was the winner of having my Dad as a slave for the day. Which young lady won? All I can say is that they quickly became a couple and a marriage which lasted 40 years. Although Mom said they got married not so much as to be together but to get them out of the dorms and into married student housing. I often wondered if that campus knew how many times it served as the backdrop of one of my favorite stories about my parents.

I have another story about my parents I learned about only a year before they passed away. It makes me smile each time I think of it and also shows the continuing love my parents had for each other. For as long as I can remember, Dad would get up in the morning and go through his morning routine. Mom would stay in bed and catch a few more winks. I was spending the weekend with then at their summer home in New Hampshire. Dad began his morning routine; get up, make coffee, feed the dogs, walk the dogs, eat breakfast. Mom, as usual, remained in bed. I went in to wake her and asked her why she didn't go downstairs and join Dad for breakfast. She smiled at me with that patient motherly smile and explained to me that Dad brought her coffee in bed every morning and that was decidedly much better than padding downstairs to the kitchen for a morning cup of coffee. Apparently, Dad had been doing this for many years and I had no idea.

Forty years of marriage for my parents and my dad was still doing something special and sweet for my mom.

Chapter Two

My father's personality was quite different from my mother's. Some say opposites attract and in this case, that adage holds true for my parents. Dad worked long hours at his job. He typically left for the office before I was awake and would return home long into the evening. As the district manager for Ryder, he was the one who had to fix any and all problems. For many years I knew I had a dad but didn't know him. He was the elusive threat Mom used "just wait until your Dad gets home." When I reached my thirties, my Dad and I often talked on the phone each morning and it quickly became a daily ritual that we both enjoyed. I felt a connection and bond with him that continued to grow.

However, when I was growing up in my parents' home, my relationship with my Dad was not a close one. The reason was that until I turned eleven years old, I don't remember spending any quality time with him. He was always working and I rarely saw him. Most of the time, Dad was already at work before my sisters and I were up for school in the morning. And, he came home at night once we had long been asleep for the night. He sporadically took some weekends off and perhaps a short vacation now and then, but for the most part, he was a virtual stranger to us.

I remember things turning around when Dad retired when I was eleven. At first, it was a major adjustment for both him and my sisters and me. Our mentality at the time was, *"Who is this man telling me what to do?"* It was annoying to have my "newfound" Dad tell me what I could and couldn't do. But, then setting the boundaries between parent and child rarely is. Once Dad began including himself in my everyday life, I began to feel more comfortable with him as a parent. For example, I was involved in many sports: gymnastics and swimming being my favorite. Dad came to a few of my gymnastic meets and he drove me and some of my teammates to swim meets and I began to think he was pretty cool. Watching my father carefully tucking each girl's long hair into the bathing caps made an impression on me. Getting up before dawn, helping me to stretch muscles; he felt it was important to involve himself in my life. I knew even then these series of events would become very important memories that would last me into old age. I began to learn how to accept this man as my Dad and love him totally.

As Dad settled into retirement and the freedom that accompanied it, he not only spent more time with his family, but he and my mother decided to move to Florida. There would be new schools, new people and definitely a new climate. Dad wouldn't have to worry about living near his job any longer!

Florida is the land of tennis and golf and Dad played both. So, it was natural that I would follow. I would start swinging a golf club when I was thirteen. I loved it although it could be very frustrating. I had a problem with not hitting every shot perfectly. When I was a teenager, there was no such thing as sports therapists.

Therefore, I had to muddle through the frustration and anger of not getting it right. One day, I was out practicing on the golf course. While I was focusing on my swing, a man came up to me and began giving me pointers and talked about "coil".

This man twisted my body around and had me swing a completely different way and then he walked away. I tried to figure out what this man meant by coil, but couldn't grasp the concept. It was no use, for some reason, I couldn't duplicate the "coil" action he referred to earlier and I couldn't hit the golf ball and by now I couldn't get back my own swing. I was frustrated with myself, which made me furious and a furious fifteen year old is not pleasant. I marched home and began shouting at my Dad and proceeded to have a fine temper tantrum. I told him about the man who changed my stroke on the golf course and he listened carefully. As I continued relaying the story, my Dad let me finish and I looked expectantly at him.

"Do you know who this man was that instructed you about the coil?" my Dad asked me.

"No, he just showed up out of nowhere and showed me how to twist my body and then I couldn't swing again!" I reiterated.

Dad nodded and continued, "Well, this guy was very impressed with you. He had been watching you for awhile before he approached you," he mentioned. By this time, he caught my interest enough so that I was listening.

"You know, I got a call from your golfing coach earlier," Dad acted as if he was going to change the subject.

"What did he want?" I inquired. "If he wants to see my golf swing, I can't do it anymore because of that man!" I harrumphed.

Dad smiled, "It turns out 'the man' you are referring to was very impressed with your skill. In fact, he called your golf coach and said he wanted to instruct you." He waited for my reaction and received none.

"That's when your golf coach called me and told me about it. That 'man' is Nancy Lopez's coach," he added with a touch of pride. In true fifteen year old style, I ignored the compliment and opportunity by giving a resounded NO, when asked if I was interested. Oh, the stupidity of youth, but bless my parents for not forcing me into the lessons!

I continued my golf lessons and played at a pretty decent level, but decided to put the clubs away after high school. It would be eight years before I would pick them up again. I don't know if Dad was saddened by that or not. I suspect he was, but never said anything. Then, one day, I tried it again and liked it. While I was working, I couldn't play much, but I did play in a twilight league and was able to shoot under 50 for 9 holes each week and maintain an 18 handicap. For a woman, that's good.

After I stopped working fulltime, I was able to practice more. I took some lessons and each summer I got a little better. I got excited when the handicap started to drop and my Dad was excited too. Mom preferred not to play golf but would join us every now and then. She was pretty good with a 7 wood, 7 iron, wedge and putter. I joked that these were the only four clubs she should bother carrying. She and I played in a few member–guest clubs together and we had a great time. She was always so proud when I won an award for long drive or any type of golfing accomplishment.

In fact, sometimes when my Dad played golf with friends, I would get the phone call that the group needed a fourth and could I come over and play? I didn't think I could possibly toss my clubs in my car any quicker! I love the course at the place where Mom and Dad lived and jumped at each opportunity to play. Mom and Dad loved hearing about my golf accomplishments. When I got my first hole in one in 2004, my first phone call was to Dad. He kidded that I wasn't supposed to do that before the old man, but I made him buy me dinner anyways.

Chapter Three

When Dad was nine, he learned he had been adopted. He didn't learn in a nice way. He learned from a bratty schoolmate who snickered and teased and thought it was oh so funny. When Dad went home to ask his parents about this, they admitted the truth. Growing up I always knew that my Dad was adopted. I asked him once if he thought about looking for his biological parents. He said no. Grandma and Grandpa had given him a wonderful upbringing with a great education and more importantly – love.

Grandma passed away when I was very young. Three weeks before her death, she cleaned out the closets, visited friends in the nursing homes and donated unused items to charity. One day, she and Grandpa came home from morning errands. Grandma went in to take a nap but never woke up. I think she knew her time was near and tied up the loose ends before her departure. I do remember she was a tiny lady. Four foot eleven and three quarters. You had to remember to add the three quarters. It was very important.

Grandpa then remarried to a wonderful lady we called Aunt Patty. He husband had passed away a few years earlier. The two couples had lived on the same road in Fayetteville, NY and the boys had played with each other growing up. I loved Patty. I loved her sense of humor and her ability to do the Sunday New York Times Crossword puzzle.

When I was young, we would visit Grandpa and Patty in Cazenovia. There was also a list of chores to around the house. Dad and I would begin each visit with a trip to the local hardware store. I think doing these projects with Dad is why I can muddle through fixing most anything at my house. I've even replaced a toilet. It's not something I want to do on a daily basis, but I have replaced a toilet.

By my early 30's, both Grandpa and Patty passed away. It was only then Dad decided to search for his biological family. Luckily, he had his original birth certificate with the mother's name. A detective quickly found the family. The mother and father had passed away but there were still siblings. Dad wrote to the siblings explaining the situation. The siblings received the letter and asked an aunt if this could be true. She said there was a child and it was possible but she didn't know anything more. Everyone else had been told the child died at birth. The daughter called Dad and suggested she and a brother fly out to the east coast to meet. She felt a blood test was in order for the dramatic claim and Dad had no problem with this request.

When the two siblings, Jackie and Ron, arrived from California and came face to face with Dad, there was no mistaking the family resemblance. It was declared that no blood tests were needed and a lost sibling was found.

My Dad's place in the biological family is interesting. He was a middle child. How did a middle child get put up for adoption as an infant? I'll tell you.

His biological Mom, Iris and Frank were married with a son. They got divorced. Iris then discovered she was pregnant. In the 1940's it was hard for a single women to care for a baby alone, let alone two babies alone. She gave the infant up for adoption. Then, Iris and Frank got back together and remarried. They had a daughter and then got divorced again. Iris then married Walter and had two sons with him. The four children never knew there was a brother out there somewhere in the world.

A few years before Mom and Dad passed away, the three of meet in California for a family visit. One of the evenings there was a family dinner. As I recall, there were two uncles, two aunts, four cousins and spouses and children. It was a great evening and I had never been surrounded by so many relatives. We visited the house where the siblings grew up. One of the uncles still owned the house and has done many improvements over the years. We also visited the San Juan Capistrano Mission Gardens where Dad had remembered being at many years ago. We then headed off to Laguna Beach to do some shopping. It was a wonderful family visit.

Chapter Four

Mom, for the most part, was the typical 60's wife of an executive. Her role in the marriage was to raise the kids and keep a clean house and deal with the in-laws. Mom tried working outside of the home when money was tight and the shoebox system was not working. The shoebox system is where you have three shoeboxes. The first is for bills that absolutely had to be paid, the electric bill, the mortgage, the car payment. The second was for the somewhat important bills like department store bills. The third was for those bills that could slide until there was enough money. The third box usually consisted of bills where Mom and Dad could run a tab like the local grocery store or the hardware store and knew if they got too far behind; the owner would say something to Grandma or Grandpa and who would then pay the tab because they were embarrassed.

One of the jobs Mom tried was Real Estate. This was a great job for someone wanting part-time employment as Mom felt strongly about being home for her husband and children, foremost.

Shortly after Mom began her realty career, she became disenchanted with the "business" side of her real estate. She was happy to show a young couple a multitude of homes that would be "just right". But, this approach didn't set well with management as they wanted to sell homes as quickly as they listed. Mom could never detach from the emotional element of guiding a young couple toward the purchase of their first new home without sacrificing her employer's turnover expectations. Needless to say, her serendipitous view of shopping for the perfect home failed to make a profit for her employer. She tried a few more jobs, but finally decided to devote herself full-time as a housewife. At least the time and energy she spent on her family was <u>her</u> timetable and no one else's.

When I decided that I wanted to become a Brownie, my mom volunteered to be the Brownie Mom. Her creativity was perfect for a bunch of first graders. My fondest memory of our many art projects was making a doll out of a Quaker Oats container. We sewed little fabric arms and legs then stuffed them with beads. Then we glued fabric to the container to make the outfit then the eyes and hair. Finally, we attached the arms and legs. My version was a mess but Mom's looked Martha Stewart perfect.

Mom's artistic creativity would become useful in the many house projects my parents would get into. Mom could take an empty room and transform it into a beautiful, comfortable living space. I was always impressed with Mom's formal rooms. They were gorgeous yet you felt like you could actually sit on the couch and rest your feet on the coffee table and not get into trouble.

Then my mother had her artistic mid-life crisis. My mom decided she needed to buy a floral shop and wanted me to run the business side of the business. If you ever want to test the family relationship, purchase a business together. Not the next generation comes into an established family business, no, a business totally new to the family. We were assured the shop was "turn- key". HA! Every owner of every business knows there is no such thing as turn-key, but we forged ahead anyway. The designers who came with the purchase hated us. I don't mean just a little bit of dislike, I mean full on despised us. We took away their business they were going to buy after they drove away some business to reduce the price to a level they could afford. They did everything and anything they could to anger us but we persevered. Within a year we had new designers working for us and the store was a much happier place to work. It also only took Mom a year to figure out she did not want to be tied down to a business. Her husband was off in Florida for the winter and she was stuck in the cold north. The day to day responsibilities were more than Mom wanted to handle. Our first full summer of ownership is when Mom informed me I would be managing the store by myself. I didn't know the first thing about flowers and the deal was I took care of the books. We decided I needed floral training and my Mom discovered a school in Ohio for floral shop owners. I headed off to three weeks of boot camp floral design school. It was the best thing I did for the business. If orders came in fast and furious, I was able to jump in and help. Our design look improved tremendously and business blossomed. With Mom off in Florida, we had a smooth running operation that was until Mom came back into town. It was similar to a hurricane. Being artistic, Mom had many great ideas for displays but did not have the attention span to complete the project. After many years of getting frustrated and having arguments with Mom, I and my employees finally learned that we only needed to wait out the hurricane. When Mom left and would typically not show up for a few weeks, we would just put everything back to the way it was. As each year passed, Mom came by the store less and less. She had moved on to other projects such as remodeling houses she and Dad would buy. Her focus was on architectural plans, colors schemes and furniture. When I felt I could not manage the store anymore, both Mom and Dad were very supportive of my decision. We closed down the business and sold the building and I was able to move on to other adventures.

One of the sad parts of Mom's life was she had Lyme disease for nearly 25 years. When we lived in Western Massachusetts, we lived on 40 acres of land. Mom did a lot of gardening each spring and summer. The summer we moved to Florida, Mom noticed a bite with rings around it. When we got to Florida she took a Lyme disease test but it had been over three weeks and the tests back in the 70's could not diagnose Lyme after three weeks. The test came back negative and Mom was sent on her way. Over the years, Mom had strange issues pop up. She would have depression for two years and then it was gone. She would have fibromyalgia for two years and then it was gone. Then Mom was diagnosed with breast cancer. For years the annual mammogram would return suspicious. Mom would go back for a six month check and the mammogram was fine. This would repeat itself for three years but then one year the two mammograms came back suspicious. A biopsy was done and it was confirmed that Mom had cancer. After weeks of visiting various doctors in Massachusetts and New Hampshire, Mom decided to have her surgery done in Miami. I remember her asking me if this was okay with me. I assured her that I felt it was the right decision. The surgery would be in December and her recovery would be in Florida where it was warm and more importantly where Dad would be. Thankfully, her surgery went very well despite being a double mastectomy and reconstruction. It took Mom months to recover but she did not have to do chemo or radiation.

In talking with friends in New Hampshire, Mom learned of a doctor in Connecticut who specializes in Lyme disease. Mom and Dad made several trips to Connecticut to meet with Dr. Raxlen. Mom was asked to list every illness and issue she

had over her entire life. The list was five pages long. After
many tests and blood samples send to various Lyme disease
centers the results were back. I drove to Connecticut with Mom
because Dad was out in South Dakota and could not be there.
The nutritionist asked Mom to bring all the supplements she
was taking. It filled a duffle bag. We met with Dr. Raxlen who
confirmed the Lyme disease. When he examined all that was in
the duffle, he said he felt the many supplements Mom was
taking were what were keeping Mom alive. The Lyme disease
should have killed her many years ago. Mom started a
progressive treatment and in eight months was finally Lyme
disease free.

It's just so sad that many years were wasted in illness because
the doctors did not believe Mom. Often, she was told it was all
in her head and would be sent on her way. It was only Mom's
perseverance and hours upon hours of research on the internet
which allowed her to survive. Unfortunately, the illness took a
terrible toll on Mom's health and body.

FAMILY AFFAIR

Chapter Five

To say that my parents gave me the love for travel would be an understatement. When my youngest sister was old enough to carry her own teddy bear which doubled as a make-shift pillow, you knew just how accustomed we all were to the world of travel.

By flying so much on our trips, we were able to take advantage of airline specials. In fact, the now defunct Eastern airlines had a great deal where you could fly unlimited for one month with at least three take offs and touchdowns. What more could we ask for?

These incentives were never wasted in our family. It was just one more great reason to fly to Tobago and Trinidad, Mexico and the Caribbean Islands.

It also gave my sisters and me a great education. Although we were away from school while traveling, learning about other countries and their culture proved to be invaluable to me. Instead of my teacher assigning me homework of daily classroom studies, he got into the spirit of things as well and assigned me to do reports on historical topics of interest of places I was visiting.

For example, in fifth grade when my family decided to take an excursion to Cozumel, I was given an assignment from my teacher to do a report on the Mayan Ruins. As part of my report, I snapped one picture after the other on my 35mm Kodak camera of the Chitiniza Ruins and the place where they sacrificed the virgins. I think I even got an A minus on this school report! There was something about being in the midst of history rather than reading about it in a textbook. It appealed to all the senses, seeing it first hand, feeling the wind and hearing the sounds of nature. It was a much better education than sitting inside a classroom staring out the window and daydreaming.

The best trips are the ones you'll remember for a lifetime. I remember when we stayed in Montserrat for two weeks and our yard seemed to attract a calf every morning. I posed barefoot with the calf one morning. Those types of moments are the ones that I love to catch on camera. It's one of my favorite photos to this day.

Even when we moved to Florida, we didn't stop traveling. One of our favorite places was going to Telluride for skiing. In the 80's the town was small and quaint with a real "home town" feel to it. I just fell in love with it. Back then, the same people that operated the ski lifts also waited staff at dinner. It was a great way to get to know a few people and it was so much fun. At the end of the week, we would have a refrigerator full of food. There was always a seasonal employee who gladly accepted everything we packed up for him. It was like giving gold to these people.

Telluride has grown significantly over the past couple of decades. The ski area has gotten much bigger, the town itself has grown and a new village has been formed right in the middle of the slopes. Still I go there every year. My parents also went to Telluride every summer for a couple of weeks to explore the area and enjoy the scenery. I've made it out there in the summer for a couple of the festivals.

While at one of the festivals, I finally took a guided jeep tour. My guide, Clay, was a great guide. We began our trip by driving out of Telluride and up Tommy Boy Road. One of our first stops was the old Tommy Boy Mine. What use to be a thriving mine town is now reduced to just a few decrepit buildings. Still, it is amazing that so many men lived so high up, digging in the mines. Our first adventure of the day was attempting to get up Imogene Pass. It had rained the evening before which meant snow in the high country. The road is narrow and step and covered with ten inches of snow. Our jeep isn't equipped to drive through snow, but Clay insists we will get to the top of the pass. Thankfully, my seat is on the upside of the mountain but I still grip onto the bar across the dash. Clay steps on the brakes, revs the engine, and then takes his foot off the brake. We go speeding up the hill about 100ft before the tires begin to spin. Clay puts the jeep in reverse and we back down the road. I was uncomfortable heading up and now I'm really uncomfortable backing down. I offered to get out and walk a path up but Clay is determined. After many times of repeating the process, speed up the hill, tires spin, back down the hill and do all over again, we finally make it to the top of Imogene Pass. It is cold, the wind is blowing but I am very happy to be standing on terra firma. The cars which followed us thanked us for clearing the way. Now I felt like I had by badge of honor and I am happy to be there. Clay and I then head down the other side to Ouray for lunch and to some of the other mines over in that area. As we head up Black Bear Road, which is dirt, rocks and ledge, we pass by a Ferrari. A shiny red Ferrari. I don't know if someone went for a joy ride and punctured the oil pan, but it was not a typical sight on the side of a mountain. We cross over the pass and I am thinking this way back to Telluride is not so bad. Then Clay's wife calls to see where we are and he tells her. I hear her say call me when you get to the bottom. I don't think anything of it until Clay says "dear Lord, thank you for this beautiful day..." I don't remember what else he said because my mind blanked. I'm thinking "What?" Clay informs me there are four switchbacks we need to get down. As we come into the first one, Clay hangs the nose over the edge. Again, I am hanging on to the bar across the dash and my feet are braced against an invisible brake. Clay then backs up the jeep so we are precariously angled downward. He cranks the wheel to the right and drives forward and the back end of the jeep drops from the upper level to the lower level. Clay then turns to me, smiles and says only three more to go. I never let go of the bar and never got any photos. I'm not sure I will ever have the courage to do that again to get photos, maybe when I'm senile and can't remember that I had already done the drive. I don't think my parents ever did that particular jeep drive. I think they would have told me and Mom would definitely have been a nervous wreck. They did do many other jeep tours and enjoyed the history of the area as much as I do which is why I continue to go back to Telluride every year

One of the perks of growing up on the southeast coast of Florida is that there is lots of water, and Mom and Dad developed an interest in boating. They had both powerboats and sailboats. Some school vacations we would load up on the sailboat and head to the Bahamas. Marsh Harbor and Little Plymouth were two of my favorite spots. There was a place called the "Blue Bee Bar" in Plymouth which had a soccer jersey from my school in the rafters. I have fond memories of these two towns.

There was a lady in Plymouth who baked the best bread in the world. We would wake up each morning to wonderful aroma of baking bread drifting across the harbor. Each day we would take the dingy to shore to buy our fresh baked bread.

When I was in college, my parent sailed the boat to the Virgin Islands. I was told I could head off with my friends for spring break and pay my way or I could join them and they would pay for everything. The choice was simple. I headed to the Virgin Island for guaranteed warm sunshine. These were some of the best trips I remember.

My freshman year of college, Mom and Dad chartered a sailboat in the Virgin Islands. It was a "bareboat" and bare it was. We had to purchase everything, soap, napkins, towels, toilet paper, bath towels, everything. The only thing the boat came with was this horrible stench. We dubbed it the "cat shit" boat. Thankfully, it never rained that week because we couldn't close any of the hatches the smell was so powerful. Regardless of the odor, Mom, Dad and I had a wonderful week. We sailed around the British Virgin Islands stopping at various islands and places. We discovered the old Dutch pirate ship which has become a floating bar. If you dare, you ride the boom out over the water and try to hang on as it comes to a crashing halt. No one is able to hang on and you get to go for a dip in the ocean. I think I consumed more rum that week with my parents than I did all year long at college.

The next year, when Mom and Dad offered the same deal, I quickly booked my flight to St. Thomas. This year we had our own sailboat and enjoyed a wonderful week without a foul smell. We discovered a wonderful restaurant, The Last Resort, off Beef Island. When we boated ashore to check out the place, a call came over the radio. One of the other boaters called to say a sailboat had broken from its anchor and was drifting. Unfortunately, that sailboat was ours. The three of us ran back to the tender. I could see the sailboat drifting backwards and various boaters fending it off their own boat. We steered our dingy to the stern to the ladder. I quickly jumped up on the boat and raced down into the cabin. The sailboat had an interior oil switch which needed to be turned on before you can start the engine. I get the switch on. Dad gets to the helm and starts the engine. Mom hangs on the ladder to keep the tender from drifting away. We got the sailboat under control. We were a well oiled team of three. The efficiency in which we handled the situation would have made even veteran boaters proud.

Once we got the anchor reset and apologized to everyone around us, we had a celebratory rum cocktail which turned into another celebratory rum cocktail. By the time we got to dinner, we were a very happy family. I vaguely recall the owner playing music on a synthesizer and the food being great. The next morning Dad slept until 9am, the latest I ever recall him doing so. We did go back the next year to figure out if the restaurant was as good as we thought and it was. I really enjoyed those weeks with my parents. They were fun to be with which was one of the reasons they became two of my best

Thereare many trips that I'll always remember. But, the memories I treasure most are the ones I took with my parents. This was especially true when I was older and my parents and I related to each other as adults. It wasn't that I didn't enjoy traveling with them when I was growing up. There is specialness when you can relate to your parent as a friend and sadly, not a lot of families achieve this kind of relationship. That's why I value my relationship with my parents so much. My life was better because they were in it.

Mom and I were the ones that loved to travel most. Dad was not as thrilled with the time away from home. I used to joke that if Dad liked a place, he would buy something because he only liked to sleep in his own bed!

When I got divorced in 1999, I felt I needed a trip. A friend of a friend was organizing a trip to South Africa and

Mom and I went as roomies. Despite the fact that I learned my Mom snored, we had an amazing time together. My Mom told me years later that she was so proud that I had blossomed into a wonderful young lady. She said she realized she had done a good job when at one point, I was telling a story and it was about me and something stupid I had done. I was sharing my moment with self-deprecating humor and the entire group was laughing. Mom was so proud of me.

Later in the trip, our group was leaving for the Durban Airport to fly to Cape Town. According to our tour guide's schedule, we had 30 minutes to pack and load up but then we got the frantic call to load up. In the hubbub of tossing things together, Mom left her wallet on the bed. It wasn't until we got to the airport that she made the panicked discovery.

I had an interesting time figuring out how to call the hotel where we were staying at, but I did it. They indeed had tried to stop us before we got to the gate, but we had already passed through. The rest of the group flew to Cape Town and I rented a car so Mom and I could drive back. Instead of being distressed about the situation, we took it as an adventure! I enjoyed driving on the "wrong" side of the street and in South Africa. There, when a car comes up behind you, you pullover to the left to the outside lane at your speed and the faster car goes by then you pull back over. No cars pulling into oncoming traffic! I loved it! At times, I had to really think about it, especially when turning to the right I had to remember to stay in the left. It's a different concept, but I loved the experience.

We made it back to Muzuli Park retrieved Mom's wallet which had her passport, driver's license, credit cards and cash and nothing was taken. Everything was intact, what a relief! We also got to stop back by an elementary school we had visited the previous day and get photos of me standing in front of the sign.

We made it back to the airport, where South African Airways had held onto our suitcases for us behind the counter. They booked us on the next flight to Cape Town without any hassles, no charge for the change and no interrogation. It was very pleasant and something not found with our domestic airlines.

So, Mom and I arrived to Cape Town at dinnertime and our group had gone out to a restaurant. I asked the manager if she knew what our plans were for the next day and the manager seemed to think that it was a "down day". Mom and I decided that we did not want to sit around all day while Cape Town was right there. The manager called up a friend who was a tour guide and set us up for our next day.

We got to meet Arthur who was originally from England. He was a hoot! At eighteen, Arthur was in the Navy stationed in Cape Town. When his tour was over, he remained in Cape Town. He had seen many changes in South Africa in the 40 plus years he had been there. Our first stop was Table Top Mountain. Arthur explained that the winds usually prevented anyone from going up on the cableway in the afternoon, so it was best to go first thing.

The view from the top was spectacular. On one side, you could see Robben Island where Nelsen Mandela had been imprisoned and the other you looked down to Cape Town.

There are dassies, or rock hyrax, which live at the top of the mountain probably fed by tourists, but they are cute and funny to watch. We got pictures of us with our hair being blown by the wind. When we can down the mountain, the cableway was closed to winds and I am very happy we were able to get to the top. Art took us to a Botanical Garden for lunch and then to Area 66 for a tour.

Area 66 had been a great community with great diversity in people and religion. Like Harlem used to be but then the government decided they wanted to take over the area and build new homes for a different set of people. The only thing left standing was the community church. Luckily, residents had taken street signs, business signs and other memorabilia from the community. For various reasons, nothing was ever built in the area. In 1999 there was only the church and many empty streets.

In the 90's a few of the residents donated signs from the community back to the church. What started as a few memorabilia turned into a community wide effort. Word spread of the endeavor and more signs came back. In an effort to preserve the history, a map of the streets with locations of businesses and residences was painted on the floor of the church. People have come by and filled in names of those businesses and residences. On the walls are photos of the faces of residents who worked and lived in the area at that time. It was a beautiful yet sad place to visit.

That was our first trip together and each year, the two girls went on a trip! We traveled to Bonaire, Fiji and Canada. For Mom's 60th birthday, Dad was required to go. The three of us went to Panama and Costa Rica on a small ship cruise. We cruised the Panama Canal, visited the Darien Jungle and hiked in parks and national forests.

At the end of each day, we would head back to the ship and the crew members would stand there with a tray of fresh baked cookies. Dad loved those chocolate chip cookies and it was our treat for slogging through the jungle, all hot and sticky.

After the cruise ship portion of the trip, we stayed near the Arenal Volcano which, unfortunately, was not erupting. Then we headed off to Tortuguera where you can't get there by car, only plane or boat. We got there by boat which had to travel through Nicaragua. We spent a few hours at immigration before being allowed to continue on our way.

Mom and I did try to go to Nepal together. It was a trip we both wanted to do. When I looked into trekking to Base Camp, Mom realized it was more difficult than she was prepared to handle. Mom and a girlfriend decided to head to the Annapurna area while I went to the Kumbu region. Our trips were almost at the same time, differing by only a couple of days. I arrived to Katmandu first. My group met at the Yak and Yeti. We did a couple days of orientation and touring around the city. I left an email for Mom telling her a couple of places I thought she might enjoy while there. It was interesting knowing that I was typing Mom an email while in Katmandu and Mom would read it when she got to Katmandu.

My group went off to the Base Camp of Mount Everest and a week later Mom's group went off to the Annapurnas. When I got back to Katmandu, I was happy to see an email from Mom which she had left for me when she was in Katmandu.

Jennifer Truman * 9132 victor!

My trek to Base Camp and hiking through the Kumbu
Region was the most inspirational trips I have taken. We flew
from Katmandu to Lukla airport which is literally cut into the
side of the mountain. The runway is at a 10 degree upward
angle. When the wheels touch you are immediately shot uphill.
I videoed the landing and each time I watch it, it still gives me
chills. From Lukla we began our trek up. There were fourteen
Americans, six Sherpas, six cooking crew, many porters and
one guide, Sona. Our entourage makes it was up to our first
camp site. We are all looking at our tents trying to figure out
how we are possibly going to sleep that night. Some partake in
a beer in one of the lodges; others savor the flavor of Pringles
which were discovered in one of the stores. We are all tired
from our first day at altitude and hiking and sleep comes
quickly. The next day we are awoken by two kitchen girls
bringing tea and a bowl of hot water to each of our tents. We
quickly learn this is the morning routine and it becomes
something you look forward to enjoying. Our next day gets us
to Namche Bazaar. It is this day we discover our guide, Sona,
has a wicked sense of humor. When asked how much farther to
go, Sona would reply "as far as my nose." Is the hike today
difficult? Piece of pie was the reply. How much altitude do we

gain today? A little bit up and then some down, he would retort. There were many more of these which Sona had practiced on many trekking groups over the years. Each one still made us groan but Sona was a wonderful guide.

When I asked Sona a question about a village, he was pleased I was interested in more than just arriving at Base Camp. Each day Sona would give me a history lesson of the area we were hiking through. A few of the other members of the trip realized what was happening and our little group hung together in the back of the pack listening to stories of the area by someone very prominent in that area.

One of the most amazing aspects of the trip was walking beneath the mountains. While we were walking at fourteen thousand feet, we would still be looking up ten thousand feet to the peaks. The entire area is beautiful, not just Mt Everest. The people of the area have a special peacefulness and inner beauty. I was lucky to have my tent near Sona's tent many nights. I had the privilege of listening to Sona's morning and evening mantra. I definitely affected me for the better. Besides getting to Base Camp and the top of Kala Pattar, I found a spiritual calmness within myself. I truly believe this calmness is what allowed me to deal with the intense situation I would be faced with in only four years.

CHAOS AT 3,000 FEET

~~~

Chapter Eight

Afew years ago, I was puttering around my house in New Hampshire, I began to feel a bit strange as my thoughts suddenly turned to my parents. Even though we had gotten to the point where we talked daily on the phone, it wasn't the same type of feeling of just calling to say hello. I tried to put it out -of my mind, but the feeling wouldn't go away. *That's it, I'm calling to see if everything is okay*, I told myself.

I called my parents who were with friends in Telluride and Mom answered the phone. After we exchanged hellos, Mom revealed that she was waiting for a phone call from Klaus at the hospital. It appeared that a good friend of the family, Ingrid; had been slammed into by a snowboarder and fell unconscious. She was rushed to the hospital and I could hear in my mother's voice the anxiety and concern as she sat helplessly by the phone for news about her friend.

Luckily, Ingrid is fine and is the same beautiful, wonderful lady we all love so much. I always said when I grew up; I want to be just like Ingrid. In my case, that would mean growing 3 inches and developing *an Australian accent!*

So, I have learned to pay attention to my gut feelings. When I felt an overwhelming feeling come over me, I knew I had to call Mom and Dad who were in Wyoming visiting friends. Over the years, I had trained them to check their cell phone at least once a day for instances such as this. However, the ideal situation was for them to have it on their person when they were away. I can track down people with the best of them, but this way was so much easier.

Nonetheless, once Mom answered the cell phone, she seemed puzzled.

"How did you already find out?"

"Find out what?" I became confused as if I entered the conversation either too early or too late.

"Bob fell off his bike, broke his neck and died," she blurted. I was dumbfounded. She continued to explain that the grandkids had biked ahead and came back when Grandpa wasn't with them and that's when they found him. The sense of loss was profound. The friends my parents were with also knew Bob. It was a sad time for everyone.

As one might imagine, Mom and Dad were very upset, but my father was particularly shaken by the news. In fact, he couldn't speak to me on the phone. It was decided that they would fly back to New Hampshire and on Monday we would fly to New York for the funeral of their dear friend. My father is a very skilled pilot and often flew from destination to destination when possible.

I called Dad around 9am to see what the game plan would be. Dad wanted to fly out by 2pm to arrive in New York before dusk. Plans were made that he would pick me up around 1:30pm and then we would head to the airport. It was around noon and I had packed my bag and was puttering around the house. As I was tidying a few things, the phone rang.

"Your Mom isn't going to be ready on time. We're going to be a little late, so just watch for us, ok?"

I could tell from the sound of his voice he was extremely exasperated with my mother. If there is one quality that sums up my father, he is extremely punctual and being late is just not in his vocabulary. After we hung up, I could imagine the scene at my parents' house. Dad would be pacing the floor while Mom is gathering and packing her things just so, with an intermittent reminder of "Dani! Come on!" serving a dual purpose to hurry my mother and act as a snoozing alarm clock.

~~~

As I fidget waiting for my parents, I glance outside the window and see their car pulling into my driveway. I took a look at my watch and saw that it was 1:45pm and wasted no time in grabbing my bag and getting into the car. We were already late and I didn't want to bear the brunt of Dad's temper for being tardy!

We are headed to Laconia Airport which is where Dad shelters his plane when he is in New Hampshire. Dad begins his pre-flight check while Mom and I get the bags out of the car and to the plane. As we are doing this, Mom misjudges the location of the aileron[2] on the plane and hits her head causing a loud "thunk." Dad and I both look at her in surprise. Mom is holding her forehead wincing in pain, and Dad gives his typical shake of the head.

I go over to Mom and look at her forehead, which is quickly forming a bruised lump. I decide to drive over to the convenience store to get some ice for Mom and also offered to get some sodas.

When I return to the plane, it's all packed and the preflight check is done. There's only one thing left to do and that is to hop in and sit in the co-pilot seat. Mom feels safe when I sit up front since I have some knowledge of the basics of flying. This also gives her some time to sit in the back and read

---

[2] Aileron – www.thefreedictionary.com/, Two movable flaps on the wings of an airplane that can be used to control the plane's rolling and banking movements

her magazines without worrying what is going on in the cockpit.

Just like clockwork, Dad fires up the engine and calls down to air traffic control for permission to leave. Seeing Dad go through his checklists and procedures is similar to seeing a watch work with precision and timing. He is also very cautious and when he flies the plane for more than just to "exercise" it, he flies what aviation professionals term, "flight following" which means that Air Traffic Control (ATC) is following you as you cross the country. The pilot is assigned a squawk number that is dialed into the radio. Dad will get these numbers and other pertinent information he needs for the flight. He is in a hurry because he only has a window of time to use that information, otherwise, he will have to re-file the flight plan and start the process all over again. Re-doing a process simply goes against the grain of an efficient and organized pilot.

Chapter Nine

Dad is hustling the plane down the taxi way which seems a bit odd to me, but I assume that he is trying to get back on schedule. I almost said something to him, but decided it would probably be better to keep my mouth shut.

We get to the run-up area and Dad goes through the procedures like I've seen him do every other time. I look off to my right and don't see any planes in the flight pattern [3] and inform Dad. Instead of turning around 360 degrees, he decides to stay in place [4]. I find this to be very odd, but I don't say anything, giving Dad the benefit of the doubt. I also didn't want to disturb him during takeoff as I have taken some piloting

---

[3] http://blog.aopa.org/letsgoflying/?p=69, the traffic flow prescribed for aircraft at, taxing on, or taking off from, an airport.
[4] http://blog.aopa.org/letsgoflying/?p=69, Traffic pattern operations at an airport are used to keep airplanes from approaching from every direction. Traffic patterns become uniform and consequent.

lessons and know that talking can disturb the pilot's concentration and that can be a very bad thing.

Dad pulls out onto the active runway and stops the plane. While he has the brakes on, he begins to throttle up. Again, I don't want to break his concentration, but feel that this is not the "normal" procedure for him. The airport in Florida that he uses is a much smaller runway and requires that a pilot become airborne that much sooner. But, in this New Hampshire airport, the runway is over 5,000 feet long.

Yet, I know sometimes he likes to practice short takeoffs, so I remain silent. The plane is throttled up and Dad lets go of the brake. As we are traveling down the runway, at liftoff speed, Dad pulls back the yoke and we are airborne. I settle back into my seat and a short time later, I notice that we are crabbing[5] to the right.

---

[5] http://www.flightsimbooks.com/ffs/glossary.php
Crabbing: A condition of flight in which, due to the direction of winds aloft, the aircraft is moving somewhat sideways through the air but following a straight line in relation to the ground. Named after the manner in which crabs move.

I've flown with my Dad enough to know how precise he is about flying. Everything is done by the book and accordingly to the flight lessons of my Brother-in-Law, who was also my Dad's flight instructor. So, I become a little concerned at the small inconsistencies in his flying skills, yet all the other steps and procedures that were taken to get into the air was perfect as always when Dad is the pilot. *It's got to be that he felt hurried,* I mused to myself.

As we leave Laconia Airport and head west, we cross over Lily Pond then Paugus Bay. I feel that it's okay to speak now and ask if Dad if he wants his soda. He doesn't respond. I tap my mike on the head set to make sure it is working and get the bay noise in my ears and try tapping him on the right arm. He turns to me and has a dazed look on his face. Instead of reacting, I remembered another quality my Dad is known for is having a wicked sense of humor which usually results in a practical joke. A typical example is when he packs a dozen golf balls under the car seat of some poor unsuspecting friend and watch them drive away. The poor friend would step on the brake and all these golf balls would roll forward under the driver's foot, gas and brake pedal! One friend bemoaned that it took him a month to find all those darn things! So, when Dad looked at me with a dazed look, I automatically assumed that he was joking around with me.

A moment passes and his expression doesn't change. "What's wrong, Dad?" There still isn't a response. At this point, I look back to Mom and she looks up from her magazine at me.

"What's wrong?"

"I don't know," and watch Mom making her way forward to be between me and Dad. She taps him on the arm like I did and Dad looks at her with the same dazed look. At this point, we know something was very wrong, but didn't know what.

For a split moment, I'm stunned as the situation was starting to sink in. Dad wasn't pulling a prank and we're 3,000 feet in the air without a pilot. At this point, I feel as though I am going on remote control. I grab hold of the yolk to take control of the plane. We are still growing altitude though the altimeter says we're only at 4,000 feet above sea level. I push the yoke forward to level off the nose, but I find it difficult to do so. It felt like minutes were ticking by as I fought to keep the plane from gaining altitude, but I'm sure it didn't really take that long. Finally, a lesson from my brother-in-law suddenly penetrated my brain. I spun the wheel forward and that eased the pressure on the nose of the plane. In the midst of these moments, my insecurities and less than ideal flight instruction began flooding my memory.

***

Chapter Ten

I didn't take flight instructions from my Brother-in-law like my dad did, though I wish I had. If I had, I may actually have gotten my pilot's license. I took lessons from a local instructor and had a difficult time learning the basics. I'd pancake[6] the landing every time. I did well on taking off and holding altitude, but it was the landing that I had trouble mastering. I just didn't feel comfortable attempting a solo landing without an instructor.

To give some background on my flying experience, the reason I was taking lessons was that Dad bribed me. He said that if I got my license, I could use the plane. At that time, he had a beautiful Mooney that looked like a little rocket ship compared to the 180 Cessna Warrior I was currently flying. How could I turn down the offer? So, one summer I flew; but still wasn't confident enough to solo at the end of the summer. I

---

[6] http://www.aeroplanemonthly.co.uk/glossary/PQ_news_70047.html
Pancaking: Landing an aeroplane in a stalled condition so that it has an abnormally high rate of descent or an abnormally low forward speed.

went to Arizona for the winter and looked into flying there, but all the airports were near Phoenix Airport and tower controlled[7] and I was nervous because I had never piloted a plane in tower controlled airspace.

It took a few months to discover a smaller airport a few towns away. It had a tower, but it was smaller and far enough away from the Phoenix airport. I began my flying lessons with an instructor by the name of Matt. Our first time in the sky, he throttles back the engine and asks, "What now?" Rather than say I didn't know, I quipped, "Panic?" He let me know that my reply was incorrect. I finally told him that I didn't know. Truthfully, back in New Hampshire emergency landings had not been part of the lesson plan. He looked at me with amazement that I didn't know what to do. Thankfully, Matt showed me what to do and going forward, emergency landings were part of the lesson each flight.

As I practiced flying over a farm field with my instructor, I spotted a man on a tractor who kept an anxious eye

---

[7] http://forums.flyingmag.com/showthread.php?t=1292 A tower controlled airport is staffed with air traffic controller(s) who communicate with the tower and deal with traffic patterns

on my aircraft! My practices consisted of flying only 20 feet above the land in a side slip before throttling back up and heading for the skies. Then, with the help of a nice 20 knot head wind, I finally made a perfect landing. Matt stated he did not know why I wasn't already soloing. He felt the time had come. The following week I was supposed to go for a check ride with Matt's boss. But, the boss became ill and then it was time for me to leave Arizona to head back to New Hampshire. I wasn't able to do my solo.

Needless to say, upon returning to New Hampshire I was feeling pretty confident about my newly honed flying skills. I took another lesson from my previous flight instructor and as I was coming in for my landing, for some reason, my flight instructor jumped forward and nearly grabs the yolk. At this point, my attention went from the runway to her and I performed another beautiful pancake. When I got out of the plane, I was pissed. I called my brother-in-law and angrily explained what happened in my lesson. He agreed to go flying with me.

A few days later, my brother-in-law and I drove to the airport to have a practice flight. We did the preflight check and I was in the pilot's seat ready to fly. I had a great take-off and coasted until my brother-in-law was ready to suggest some maneuvers for me.

"Okay, do you know how to balance the plane?"

One look at my puzzled face and he knew the answer. He showed me the trim wheel on the floor of the plane between the pilot and co-pilot seats. This had been shown to me on the first day of my lessons and then never mentioned again.

"You can roll the trim wheel forward and backwards to help level the plane, see?" I listened carefully and was able to follow his instructions. "Once you are at your altitude you can level the balance of the plane, you pretty much do not need to touch the yolk," he continued. I was listening closely and offered, "So, it's like if there is a disturbance and the plane will level itself back out." He nodded and we continued flying for a short time after that.

Soon, we head back to Laconia Airport for the dreaded landing. I could feel my confidence starting to sink.

"My first lesson I was shown how to land and that was it," I replied. My brother-in-law took the yoke and demonstrated how it was done. As I watched, I felt as if a light bulb went off in my head. We took off again and flew for a short time and then got into position for landing the plane. I was anxious to try my landing with my newly acquired knowledge. I was almost surprised that I landed the plane so well. I didn't take any more lessons because I didn't like my flight instructor and wasn't brave enough to ask to take lessons from another instructor.

***

I was finally able to level the plane and I looked over to see Mom unbuckling the seat belt for Dad and then attempting to lift him out of the seat, without success. Anyone who has flown in a commercial plane has experienced how difficult it is to get in and out of the passenger seats. Imagine being hunched over and having someone try to move you out of the seat. I wasn't sure what Mom was trying to accomplish by moving Dad except to perhaps try and attend to him? Or try to get in the pilot seat to try and help me. I'll never know her reasoning; all that I knew for sure is that Mom was trying to lift a 200 pound man while I was attempting to get control of the plane.

Meanwhile, I made the most important call anyone can make.

Chapter Eleven

T he following is an actual transcription of my conversation with the tower at Laconia Airport, provided by the FAA.[8]

FOIA 2004-007726NE N9132V 8/9/04 UTC

Flight Assist A90-04-001

Boston Consolidated TRACON

Sector East 1956-1958 UTC

Flight Data Manchester 1958-2022 UTC

TRUMAN: Manchester, Manchester this is November... um... 9132 Victor the pilot is not well and we have to go back to Laconia please help me.

I completely forgot that I should have said "Mayday Mayday!" I knew I wanted to convey to the person on the other

---

[8] Federal Aviation Administration US government

Jennifer Truman * 9132 victor!

end of the mike that my situation was serious and I wanted them to stop drinking coffee and pay attention. My mom was assisting Dad and I had control of the plane and I didn't think things were too bad. When the words came spilling out of my mouth, I was more upset than I had first thought. My voice was very shaky.

TOWER: November 99132 Victor, Boston approach what (is) your position right now?

TRUMAN: We just left Laconia we were headed west and probably... um... over I93.

TOWER: Okay, what was your... do you have a problem right now? Is that what you're request is.

TRUMAN: The pilot of the plane is not well... he's not... he's very...I don't know what...I can't tell you what happened he is not responding at all.

Breathe, Jennifer, just breathe. It's going to be okay.

Jennifer Truman * 9132 victor!

TOWER: Roger November 99132 Victor. Squawk 5171.

TRUMAN: 5171. I will try to change that over. Squawking 5171.

I did change the transponder to 5171, but I didn't switch it to Mode C. Mode C allows the Air Traffic Control to see not only your position, but also your altitude. I'm not sure it had been turned on at the start of the trip.

At this point, I get transferred over to Ken Hopf in Merrimack, New Hampshire, although I did not know his name at the time.

TOWER: November 99132 Victor this is Boston approach. How you doing?

TRUMAN: I'm fine, my father who is the pilot of the plane is not really responding and cannot talk very well... and he's not doing well.

TOWER: Okay November 99132 Victor. Do you have any experience in flying the plane yourself, ma'am?

TRUMAN: I have flown a Warrior; I have never flown a Malibu.

TOWER: Okay, Well… um…they're very similar…and we're going to do the best we can to help you. Can you ident…Are you familiar with any of the function of the airplane like the transponder and stuff?

TRUMAN: Um…the transponder, yes…the code…frequency code.

TOWER: Okay November 99132 Victor, yes… we have a good reply of your transponder. What would be your request? Are you familiar with the Laconia airport at all?

TRUMAN: Ah yes, I just took off from the Laconia airport and I'm actually not too far away from it right. I'm way too high right now. But I need to get the plane down on the floor and I need an ambulance to meet us there.

Jennifer Truman * 9132 victor!

TOWER: Okay, November 32 Victor. How many other souls are on board the airplane and how much... I am assuming you have plenty of fuel since you were on route somewhere?

TRUMAN: We were in route to Utica and we have plenty of fuel and my mother's on board and she's trying to help my father right now but he's kinda swatting her away.

TOWER: Okay, very good, and is he going to inhibit your ability at all to fly the airplane?

TRUMAN: He has no ability at all.

I misunderstood the question. I thought Ken was asking if Dad had any ability.

TOWER: Okay very good. November 32 Victor can you...are you able to turn the airplane to a heading?

Will you be able to turn the aircraft to a heading of three-three-zero, that's would be a left turn.

TRUMAN: I can turn the plane to three-three-zero, hang on. I got it.

I hadn't realized the plane was flying on a heading so far north. Taking off from Laconia, you are going almost due west. Now I am heading north-northwest.

TOWER: Very good, turn the plane to a heading of three-three-zero and advise me when you're on that heading.

TRUMAN: I think I'm about three-three-zero. Sorry- hang on.

TOWER: Okay November 32 Victor that's fine – just advise me on that heading and I don't know how familiar you are with that plane. Do you know how to slow the airplane up, reduce the throttle settings, and prepare the aircraft for landing?

TRUMAN: No, this one...no I haven't flown this plane. I know we have landing gear that I have to get down. I can see it but...I... I... it's going to take me a little bit... um... to go through it, so no I don't know much about the Malibu.

TOWER: Okay November 32 Victor, I see that you have made that turn here so that reassures me that you have control of the airplane. And I would like you to maintain your present altitude and continue your turn to a heading of two-seven-zero I'm going to try to give you a little bit more space so that maybe we can work through some of the details of preparing the aircraft for arrival. So turn left to a heading of two-seven-zero.

TRUMAN: Two-seven-zero maintaining altitude.

Now I am flying the plane west, still away from Laconia airport.

Jennifer Truman * 9132 victor!

TOWER: And... November 32 Victor I our effort here to try to ascertain what would be the best thing for you, do you think landing at Laconia would be the best thing for you versus some other larger airport?

TRUMAN: Ah, Laconia is long enough to land the plane. It's like over five thousand feet and Laconia would be the best and an ambulance to Laconia hospital would be the best.

TOWER: Okay Very good. We're already speaking with people on the ground as far as arranging an ambulance to arrive at the Laconia airport. Um November 32 Victor, are you...do know where the gear selector know is?

TRUMAN: Gear selector knob? No.

TOWER: Okay the landing gear. First thing is November 32 Victor, there is some traffic out there at your one o'clock position and three miles. The altitude on the aircraft that is converging with you is 3700 feet.

TRUMAN: Okay – I have him on the radar.

TOWER: Okay November 32 Victor just keep an eye on that there and um...on the instrument panel, generally somewhere around the center of the console there's a knob kinda looks like a... sometimes it looks like a lifesaver. You know it's kinda round. Has a round edge. Like a big circle about an inch and a half in diameter and the gear selector is attached to that.

TRUMAN: Is that the landing gear down?

TOWER: Yes, that would be the landing gear down lever. Do you see that?

TRUMAN: Affirmative.

TOWER: Okay November 32 Victor. Can you tell me your altitude? I'm not receiving your mode C at present. This is the mode that allows Air Traffic Control to see the altitude.

TRUMAN: I'm at 4700 feet.

TOWER: Okay November 32 Victor Roger. And turn left at a heading of one-eight-zero.

TRUMAN: Left to one-eight-zero.

Now we are heading south.

TOWER: And November 32 Victor do you have a good view of the airspeed indicator from your position in the cockpit?

TRUMAN: Yes, I have a...yes...I have one right in front of me.

TOWER: Okay very good. Now you say you're familiar with flying the airplane and in the respect... well you are not familiar with flying the Malibu but you have flown a Cherokee in the past. Correct?

TRUMAN: I have flown a Warrior, a Piper Warrior.

TOWER: Okay...a piper Warrior..okay.. one of the things we are looking at right now is the wind at Laconia is basically out of the West 2-9-0 at 7 and gusting to 1-6. So, the best thing would be to bring you in to the airport from the eastern side and have you arrive to the airport straight in to runway 2-6. Do you concur with that?

TRUMAN: I concur. That's how we took off. Concur.

TOWER: Okay very good. Now, one of the things is I want to try to go through is ensure that you have the ability to control the airplane and slow the speed up. You have the throttle control, you understand how that works?

TRUMAN: Yes, I have the throttle and the prop RMP and the mixture.

TOWER: Okay November 32 Victor. And at present it looks like you're eastbound. If you would, could you fly heading of zero-nine-zero?

TRUMAN: Zero-nine-zero

Off mike, I begin questioning Mom. "Mom, where is the landing cheat sheet? Is the cheat sheet on the plane?" The cheat sheet is a card that helps a non-pilot land the plane. It has information such as the landing speed, how to operate the flaps, how to apply the brakes and how to control the throttle. Mom stops fiddling with dad and gets out the oxygen mask. She tries to place it on dad but he wouldn't have anything to do with it. My turn has us flying east. This has us flying past the Laconia airport.

TOWER: November 32 Victor one of the things that we're trying to work with is the fact, well...actually the fact you are on the clearance delivery frequency should help us a lot because radio communications, sometimes we lose on the other side of the mountain but because you're on the clearance delivery frequency, that's going to help a lot in maintaining two-way communication with you. Continue on a heading of zero-niner-zero this is a vector for a downwind for runway two-six at Laconia.

TRUMAN: Okay, continuing for downwind for two-six Laconia.

"Mom, where's the cheat sheet?"

Jennifer Truman * 9132 victor!

TOWER: Okay November 32 Victor, that previous issue target is still out there he's at your eleven o'clock now about a mile and a half, southeast bound altitude indicates 3100. It will be passing beneath you.

TRUMAN: Okay, I have him on the radar but I haven't spotted him but I will keep an eye out for him. Thank you.

About 50 seconds pass before we speak again

TOWER: Okay November 32 Victor as far as extending the landing gear and flying the airplane would you like to try to practice that before we set you up for arrival at Laconia.

TRUMAN: Um..yeah…well, I think once I get into…I think I'm down at landing gear where I can put it down and leave it down.

Jennifer Truman * 9132 victor!

What I was trying to say was I felt my airspeed was slow enough that the landing gear could go down and not damage the plane, but obviously that thought didn't come out of my mouth the right way.

TOWER: Okay November 32 Victor, so you would like to extend the landing gear at this point and just continue flying the airplane with the gear extended?

TRUMAN: That's affirmative.

TOWER: Okay November 32 Victor, Roger. Why don't you extend the landing gear now and just give me advice when you have three green light indications.

TRUMAN: Well, I have three green lights so, the landing gear must…he must not have put up the landing gear to begin with. So, I have three green lights right now. Left, middle and right.

TOWER: Okay very good. So you are flying the airplane with gear extended. Okay very good and as far as operating the throttle... this particular model...this is not a turbine aircraft is it? It's a regular gas engine?

TRUMAN: Regular gas engine, yes.

TOWER: Okay very good. Well, you are going good flying heading of zero-niner-zero. I'm going to continue you on that heading for probably a few more miles. I'm trying to work several different issues as far as our radar coverage and I want to insure you have a good visual on the airport before I allow you to descend down any further.

"Mom... Mom...Mom" I glance back to see mom is kneeling on the floor of the plane and bent over the seat behind me. I reach my hand back and tap her arm. I get no response. I turn around to see mom looking up at me. She has the oxygen mask over her nose and mouth.

She looks at me with a pain in her eyes. She is conveying to me that she can hear what I'm saying but can't move or function and doesn't know what is wrong. I quickly realize that there is something horribly wrong with Mom. I did not know that was going to be the very last time I would ever see Mom's eyes open.

TRUMAN: Um…I need to get down to…my mother is also…my mother is…something is really weird… she's flopping over like a doll now. I got two of them that are just…um…um… both of them are…are flopping over.

TOWER: And November 32 Victor, what was that last part you said?

TRUMAN: My mother is also not responding to me.

TOWER: Okay very good. November 32 Victor turn left to a heading of zero-six-zero.

TRUMAN: Zero-six-zero

Jennifer Truman * 9132 victor!

TOWER: Now we are flying northeast still away from the airport. And November 32 Victor, can you open some kinda window in the airplane? I don't know if you are suffering from some type of carbon monoxide poisoning in the aircraft.

TRUMAN: Ah...hang on a moment.

TOWER: Yeah, open some kind of vent. Open the...ah...side vent or something.

TRUMAN: The side vents are open.

TOWER: Okay, the side vents are open. Okay thank you. November 32 Victor, are you able to descend the plane down to 4000 ft?

TRUMAN: Ah...descending to 4000.

TOWER: Okay November 32 Victor. So, you should be over the lake at this point. Is that correct?

TRUMAN: Correct, I'm almost to Wolfeboro.

TOWER: Okay very good. So, you're very familiar with the area, so know if you continue north bound from here maybe a heading of three-six-zero you're gonna see Wolfeboro and then the Laconia airport will be off to your left side by about...oh...I'm gonna say about your nine o'clock and about seven to eight miles.

TRUMAN: Correct. I have the Laconia airport in sight.

TOWER: Okay November 32 Victor, Roger. With the gear extended why don't you start your descent down now to...oh say... 2500 feet.

Jennifer Truman * 9132 victor!

TRUMAN: Descending to 2500 feet.

TOWER: November 32 Victor, one of the most important things is, you remember, when the airplane goes get on the ground is...and I'm assume you're familiar with this since you've flown a Cherokee before, is to use the brakes as soon as the airplane lands.

TRUMAN: Okay. Use the brakes as soon as I land.

TOWER: Yes, just don't let the plane start freewheeling down the runway. You don't want to lose control of it. Once the airplane touches down on the runway, and based on your experience on flying a Cherokee before just keep it aligned with the centerline when it does land but do insure that you step on the brakes and slow the plane down to a complete stop and then pull the mixture out as soon as the airplane gets on the ground and stop the engine because you don't want to have the engine running or have it impede anyone's ability to access the airplane and provide assistance to your parents.

TRUMAN: Thanks. I...I understand.

Which, actually I didn't. At this point I am concentrating on descending and landing the plane, something I was not very good at. I hoped Ken would repeat this information so I didn't have to retain it in a brain that was overloading at the moment.

TOWER: Okay very good. So, November 32 Victor you have the airport in sight and you are in a gradual descend. At this point would you like to add 10 degrees of flap?

TRUMAN: Um...flap...I...

TOWER: Okay if you are not familiar with the flaps then don't be too concerned with that. Ah...say your airspeed

TRUMAN: Airspeed one-three-oh

TOWER: Okay why don't you start pulling the throttle back a little bit. Maybe a couple of hundred, well do you get by manifold pressure on that?

TRUMAN: Your guess is as good as mine.

TOWER: Okay. Reduce the manifold pressure to about twenty inches and start slowing the airplane down.

TRUMAN: Okay, manifold pressure. Where is that?

TOWER: Actually, why don't you just pull the throttle back. The black knob. Pull the black knob back out so the engine starts to slow down a little bit. Just listen to it by sound.

TRUMAN: Airspeed down to one-two-zero

TOWER: Okay very good. Just pull the throttle back a little bit more and start slowing the airplane. Now, when the airplane does land you are probably going to be going very fast so, like I said, just apply the brakes as soon you can get the airplane...as soon as the airplane touches down on the runway. You're about 2 miles from the airport. Are ya able to reduce the throttle a little bit more and just slow the airplane up?

TRUMAN: Alright...I'm almost at...ah... minimal throttle here.

TOWER: Well, if the airplane starts to ah...you know...you want to keep a good look on the airspeed indicator. You don't want to slow down too much because you don't want to stall the airplane but you do want to slow it down the best you can so when it gets on the ground, you're not going way too fast.

TRUMAN: Do you know what the…um… landing speed is for this plane?

TOWER: I have no idea what the landing speed is but I wouldn't slow any slower than a hundred knots.

TRUMAN: Okay. No slower than a hundred knots.

TOWER: And just so you know, everyone there is waiting your arrival.

TRUMAN: Thank you.

Jennifer Truman * 9132 victor!

I can see there is a plane on the taxi way and about to come out on the runway. I'm thinking "What the…? Doesn't this A-hole know I've got a problem?" I watch him take off. I'm thinking, I'm landing this plane whether the plane is off the ground or not. There is a rule that only one plane can be on the active runway at a time, but if he hasn't taken off, there will be two planes on the active runway and I don't care. It does take off to the west and I don't have to worry about that. Dad starts trying to grab the controls. I have to reach over and grab his hands. "Dad, Dad, I got it. It's Okay. I got it."

TOWER: And 32 Victor, how far are you from the runway right now?

TRUMAN: I…ah…it's in sight. I…um…maybe a half a mile.

TOWER: Okay very good. So, you're lined up with the runway, you've got your hand on the throttle. Just pull the power back a little bit more if you need to, to slow the airplane up. Just line it up with the center of the runway. How is your altitude looking?

Jennifer Truman * 9132 victor!

TRUMAN: I'm at one-seven-zero and descending.

I meant to say one-seven-zero-zero but I am getting very worried about the landing. Okay Jennifer, you can do this. You really can do this!

TOWER: November 32 Victor, how far from the field now?

TRUMAN: A couple of hundred yards.

TOWER: Okay. Just advise me when you are on the ground.

Now – count out thirty seconds. One…two…three…-…thirty. That's how long Ken had to wait on the other end. Meanwhile, this is what I have to deal with. I'm coming in to the runway, lined up on the centerline. My airspeed is one hundred knots. All I'm thinking is – please Jennifer, just get this plane down. I can see the fire truck. It's sitting to the right on the taxi way. I want to stop this plane before the fire truck. I'm almost down; I'm pulling back on the yoke, getting the nose up in the air so I don't pancake the landing. Two wheels touch and the plane goes back up in the air. My dad, who's seat belt had been undone by mom, flops forward and back. I have to shoot my hand out over to him to keep him from falling. I apologize out loud to Mom and Dad. Then I start swearing at myself. "Okay, Jennifer. Get this fucking plane on the ground now!" When the wheels came down again, there was no way they weren't staying down. I pulled back on the yoke and almost couldn't see the end of the runway. Well, it worked. Those tires stayed down.

TRUMAN: On the ground.

TOWER: November 32 Victor and apply the brakes. Have you come to a complete stop?

TRUMAN: Yes, I'm at a stop. Thank you very…here's the fire department. Thank you very much.

TOWER: 32 Victor, Roger. Nice work. Make sure that you stop the engine. Pull the mixture out, the red knob, all the way out.

TRUMAN: Engine has been cut. Thank you.

TOWER: Okay. Thank you. Have a nice afternoon.

TRUMAN: You too. Thank you very much.

End of taped transcript.

    At this point, all I can think of is getting the door to the plane open. Many small planes have the door on the right side of the plane over the wing. The Malibu has the door on the left side in the rear. I unbuckle my seatbelt and climb over Mom. I tell Mom and Dad to hang in there. Help is on the way. I open the door and stumble out. The fire truck is on the way over. The first person I see is Bruce. I know him. He was married to my friend, Donna Duncan and they are still friends. He sees me and comes over to wrap his arms around me. I collapse is his arms. He told me he had no idea it was me in the plane. I was overwhelmed with a mixture of relief, panic and emotional exhaustion.

I remember hanging on to my friend and watching the crew swarm the plane. Before I have surfaced from my hug, the firemen have already gotten Mom. I turn to see them take out Dad. Once Mom and Dad were out, a fireman jumped in the plane and headed up to the cockpit to take a carbon monoxide reading. He comes back to the doors and informs us the readings are normal. One of the guys I know from Skybright has come over to me. I asked him to take care of the plane and he told me he would move the plane to inside the hangar. Before I left, I grabbed Mom and Dad's wallets and then was given a ride to Dad's car. When I drove out of the airport, I happen to be right behind one of the ambulances. I stayed right on the bumper of the ambulance as we drove to the hospital.

I remember thinking, *Okay, now they'll get medical attention and they'll be fine.* I was ready for this horrible day to be over. I did not know that the nightmare was just beginning.

RACING AGAINST TIME

~~~~

Chapter Twelve

It seemed strange to me to be racing Dad's car behind an ambulance when only moments ago, I was trying to land a plane. The one thing I was focused on now, was to get to the hospital so the doctors could attend to Mom and Dad.

I did my best to keep my speed up so that I was right behind the ambulance, but when we got to a red light I just didn't feel comfortable making the left turn. So, I stopped and I remembered that I should call my sister who lives in the next town over. I called her at home and left a message that Mom and Dad were being taken to the hospital and that I didn't know what was wrong.

I didn't know her cell number and I struggled to think of ways to contact her and race to the hospital at the same time. I began to rack my brain, *what was the name of the business where her husband works?* I finally remembered and dialed him at work and told him what had happened. By now, I'm at the hospital which is luckily only 10 minutes from the airport.

The fireman, Bruce, who wrapped me in his arms had called Donna and told her what happened. She just happened to work at the hospital. Donna met me in the parking lot of the Emergency Room and I felt as if I staggered out of the car. Donna rushed toward me with a huge hug and leads me into the ER. She said that there was some paperwork to complete. Luckily, I was glad I had the wherewithal to grab Mom and Dad's wallet from the plane. As I am finishing up the paperwork, my sister and her husband arrive.

We are given a private waiting area and are told we can make whatever phone calls we need to on the house phone. I called my other sister in Florida to tell her what has happened. The staff told us that the Co2 levels were normal and both would be going in for CAT scans.

About 20 minutes or so, Dr. Hobson comes out to tell us that the CAT scan showed that Dad had bleeding in the brain and they felt it was best to get him to Dartmouth Hitchcock

Hospital. While my sisters and I were trying to digest that information, five minutes later, Dr. Scott comes out to tell us that the CAT scan showed the Mom had bleeding in the brain. We were in disbelief. *Could both of them have the same thing at the same time?* The doctor looked at us questioningly. Dr. Scott did not know that Dr. Hobson had just informed us of the same diagnosis. Dr. Scott left to arrange for Mom's transport to Dartmouth Hitchcock Hospital. We sat in our waiting room in shock. More paperwork had to be completed. Meanwhile, the helicopter had arrived to transport Mom to Dartmouth Hitchcock. A second helicopter was on its way to transport Dad.

In the midst of signing papers, hospital attendants prepping Dad and Mom for transport, I was in the ER having my own blood work done because of the Carbon Monoxide concern. I was not able to go out to the helipad when they airlifted Mom. My sister came in exasperated because the flight crew was asking medical questions and I wasn't there to answer them. I was able to get out to the helipad for the Dartmouth helicopter which took Dad. They wanted to know his weight, allergies and medications. I answered the questions and went back to finish my exam which felt like it lasted for an eternity, but was more likely 45 minutes in length. The staff wanted to rule out too much Co2 in my system. Thankfully, they established that my levels were fine and I was finally allowed to leave.

Chapter Thirteen

I raced home and grabbed some clothes then drove over and picked up my sister at her house. The drive-up to Dartmouth Hitchcock is about 1 ½ hours with almost no cell service the entire way.

On our way to DHMC[9] , my sister called to get an update on both parents. It was approximately 8:00pm and the doctors were looking at them. Dr. Kubata who said they were prepping Mom for emergency surgery because the pressure in her brain was building at an alarming rate. Mom was in surgery until midnight.

We get to get to Dartmouth Hospital and I have more paperwork to complete. We are finally allowed to see Dad. He's awake, but not sure what has happened. We are waiting for a room in the hospital to open for Dad so he can be transferred out of the ER.

---

[9] DHMC – Dartmouth Hitchcock Medical Center

Around 11:30pm (Mon) - Dad was moved to 4 West where he was opening and closing his eyes and giving slight responses to questions.

Approximately 12:15am (Tues) – Dr. Simmons, the neurosurgeon, spoke to me and my sister about both Mom and Dad. With Mom, there had been significant swelling in the brain and the team was hoping the surgery would alleviate the pressure. With Dad, Dr. Simmons felt he had a hypertension hemorrhage, essentially a stroke, lost mobility on his right side and has expressive aphasia[10]. We were both numb with the news. In a matter of hours, our world had been turned upside down

Approximately 1:00am (Tues) – Mom was brought to PACU[11] for recovery. Mom's nurses worked in shifts. Pam was the Night Nurse and Rhonda was the Day nurse. Each of these wonderful nurses took good care of my mother and kept me and my family aware of any news, improvements or setbacks that

---

[10] Wikipedia, http://wikipedia.org/wiki/Aphasia   Aphasia is a loss of the ability to produce and/or comprehend language, due to injury to brain areas specialized for these functions
[11] PACU -   Post Anesthesia Care Unit

my Mom was experiencing. Rhonda saw improvement in Mom in her right arm and left leg movement, so the doctors lowered the sedation level. Mom's eyes were less dilated and showed slight reaction.

While Mom was resting, Dr. Simmons came by to speak to my sister and advised that there wasn't any sign of an aneurysm but would give Mom 4-6 days to recuperate and then do another brain scan.

Approximately 1:00am (Tue): My sister and I went and saw Dad one more time before heading over to the hotel. Dad appeared to be resting peacefully with some snoring. I looked at my watch and saw that it was 1:00am and I took it as my cue to call it a day and try to rest before for a few hours before going back to the hospital.

I honestly don't know if I slept that night I Doubt I did but the exhaustion was really setting in on me. It seems that the next few days were a total blur for me.

The only thing that stands out in my mind is calling relatives and a few friends to let them know the news. On

Tuesday, my uncle and aunt from Vermont arrived along with my sister and her daughter from Florida.

11am (Tues) - Claudia, a speech therapist came by to do some evaluations. Dad was able to do a pretty good job of answering her questions. She asked him to count to 3 and he did and continued to 10 quickly. She then asked him to count to 10 slowly and he got stuck on seven and continued with a little help. She asked him more questions and tested him on recognizing shapes and pictures. He got approximately half of them correct and was stuck on the others.

It seemed that this would be the way things would be for awhile. Doctors and nurses coming in and out of Mom and or Dad's room, taking tests, checking vitals, making notes and so on. We all tried to be patient and let the doctors do what they must in order to help Mom and Dad.

Early afternoon (Tues) - Dad went in for an MRI in the afternoon and was brought back to his room afterward.

Later afternoon (Tues) - he was brought back for another MRI for contrast. I sat in a chair next to Dad's bed and did what I could do. Watch for any sign, whether good or bad, hold their hand and talk to them, read to them, anything to let them know that I was there. It seemed like this was a never-ending process, but I was happy to do it if it would help my parents recover from this.

Late afternoon (Tues) -Mom was moved to ICU #3 and as always, my sisters or I would always make a note of the nurse's name that was attending to Mom whether it was day or night shift. By early evening, Mom was taken off of morphine. She seemed to be resting comfortably.

Tuesday night - the story made the local TV news. The next day, I made a point of discussing with a case worker to have all calls routed away from the family. I figured that anyone who mattered knew my cell number. By Friday, I was told over 400 phone calls had come in to the switchboard. Unfortunately, one call did get through to the ICU and my youngest sister took the call. The next day, her phone conversation is plastered all over the Springfield news in Massachusetts. The family makes a point of not taking any calls coming through the hospital

Wednesday approximately 3am, Mom went in for in for a CT scan due to change in her reactions. She stopped reacting to stimuli and was showing signs of posturing in the extensor movement. They looked for a possible re-blood or a pressure effect but didn't see any. They gave her Mannitol to reduce the intracranial pressure.

Approximately 6am (Wed), Mom was taken for another CT scan for a point of reference. There was no further swelling but it was determined that bleeding in the mid-brain (in the brain stem) had occurred. The doctor decided they needed to go back into surgery.

7:00am (Wed) - Dr. Simmons took Mom back into surgery. Some bone was removed to give the brain room to swell and possibly let interior pressure subside. Dr. Simmons also looked around a bit more in the brain.

7:00am (Wed) – Donna Duncan calls me to let me know the story is going to be on Good Morning America. The family is in the waiting area of 4 West. Dad is going through more physical therapy and we want to be there for the results. I ask if I can turn on the TV to ABC. Everyone agrees. We all watch as Diane Sawyer introduces the next news segment about a daughter having to land a plane while both her parents were incapacitated. It cuts away to the local station, WMUR and the story showing the airport is aired. When GMA cuts back to Diane, she states "it's like something out of a movie." It was an odd feeling stating there watching the story, having lived it and then having someone else talk about the situation. I always figured that moment would remain with me and somehow change my life, but at the moment I had two very important people who needed me.

Approximately 10:00am (Wed), Dr. Simmons met with me and my sisters to discuss what happened with both Mom and Dad.

He noted that Mom's CT scans indicated that her blood vessels looked "lumpy and bumpy" not smooth, and they seemed inflamed. This is one of the reasons why she was more susceptible to pressure changes in the brain. Still, no aneurysm was detected during surgery and he doesn't think there is one.

"It's possible that she had a bloodless stroke[12]," Dr. Scott explained. "We just need to let your Mom recover from the bleeding and wait to see the results."

"Ladies, your Dad's MRI showed no blood clots. The bleeding was in the basal ganglia area (thalamus) and there shouldn't be a high chance of it happening again," Dr. Simmons explained. "I looked for AVM material vessel mestasis,[13] and didn't see that. I also didn't see any tumors. Your Dad doesn't need Cumadin [14] I feel that he will recover well, to what extent? I don't really know. We can expect improvements to be week-by-week, not necessarily day-by-day, but there are good prospects for his recovery."

---

[12] Bloodless Stroke – Lack of oxygen stroke which may have turned into a bleeding stroke.
[13] http://www.itg.uiuc.edu/ms/equipment/microscopes/afm.htm, a method of measuring surface topography on a scale from angstroms to 100 microns
[14] Cumadin – Drug used to thin blood

We sat silently mulling over what the doctor had just said and while it had a hopeful tone, I couldn't help but feel helpless and defeated as I was more than able to read between the lines.

10:30am (Wed) - A half hour later, I visited with Dad. As I was sitting next to his bed, I was able to speak with Claudia, the speech therapist regarding Dad's progress. She stated that Dad is doing better than yesterday as he could feel food on the right side of his mouth, but couldn't get it out with his tongue. She went on to detail that he got "...*8 out of 10 things right on a quiz and got stuck on "5" but could read "five"*... She continued reading his status in a matter of fact tone as I tried to wrap my mind around the fact that she is talking about my Dad. Her analysis seemed so clinical and distant as I was trying to find a morsel of good news in her findings. My attention snapped back to her analysis; "...*He has no feeling in his right arm but he can shift his weight in a wheelchair*..." and, I made notes, asked questions and focused on what I had to do next. It was my way of coping. Taking things step by step.

10:30am (Wed) – Meanwhile, one of my sisters was visiting with Mom. Her eye was swollen from the second surgery and her skin was chilly. A blanket was requested

2:30pm (Wed) – Mom goes into x-ray to check the feeding tube and make sure it had been placed correctly.

Later afternoon (Wed) - my younger sister visited with Dad. It's difficult when you must watch a member of your family struggling to recuperate from physical injury, but, when the injuries are neurological; it becomes that much more difficult. Watching our father as he became confused and frustrated about what was happening to him was gut wrenching for all of us. As she sat with him, Dad asked again what happened to him. And, again, she told him the entire story, knowing that she would probably have to retell the story many times more.

Around 3:15pm (Wed) - It was time for Dad to go to physical therapy. The nurse transported him downstairs to check his motor skills and other basic functions. We watched as they had him sit on the bed and get his own balance. Then, slowly they got him to standing.

"That's it, Mr. Truman. Great job!" the PT therapist encouraged. "Okay, let's try something different, okay? I'm going to put these cones down. Your job is to pick them up and place them here. Ready?"

Dad did the testing with the cones and was twisting and placing the cones correctly. He was doing great! Without realizing it, we all had a smile on our face as he did well with each task. After awhile, they helped him into a wheelchair and he wheeled himself around using his left and he did very well. He even maneuvered the chair through a doorway and turned around to roll back to the therapist. The fatigue on his face was beginning to show, so he was taken back to his room for rest.

4:30pm (Wed) - Later in the day, my youngest sister visited Mom and didn't notice any "posturing[15]" the entire time she was there. Mom needed blood pressure medication only

---

[15] Wikipedia, http://en.wikipedia.org/wiki/Abnormal_posturing**Abnormal posturing** is an involuntary flexion or extension of the arms and legs, indicating severe brain injury

once for that day. While the nurses were changing the sheets on the bed, they rubbed lotion on Mom's back.

"Her right eye is unresponsive and the left is slightly responsive," the nurse mentioned as she continued checking Mom's vitals. The nurses did a great job of keeping us informed of her condition.

8:00pm (Wed) -That night, Dad got a real bath and I know he felt so much better once he was cleaned up. After the bath and fresh hospital garb to wear, my youngest sister, niece and husband came to visit Dad. They were careful to ask "yes/no" questions of Dad so that he could respond. When Dad tried to ask questions, he couldn't seem to get the question out of his mouth. Fatigued and frustrated, he gave up. He seemed to recognize his granddaughter, but didn't say her name.

They visited for awhile and left when they felt Dad was getting tired. My brother-in-law casually said, "I'll see you later," and we were all surprised when he responded with the phrase, "Looking forward to it." It was those moments that kept us hopeful.

Thursday am - The next morning, the IV team put in a new IV in Mom's neck because the other ones were getting old and it was hard to find any other good veins. My sister makes a note to question Dr. Simmons; *Does Mom have arterial scoliosis?*[16]

10:30am (Thu) On my way to visit Dad I pass by Dr. Simmons. He gives me an update on Mom. Mom is stable. There have been no improvements but no deterioration. In a couple of days they will do another MRI to get finer detail. They didn't do one earlier because not enough time had elapsed to see if there had been any changes.

Thursday - Dad is responding well to therapy. His doctors feel that he is ready to be transferred to a rehabilitation center. Dad's speech is much improved and his mobility is improved. Dad could straighten out his right leg using the muscle. The right hand is starting to move a little and Dad tries to us it to assist in lifting the leg. However, if Dad leans too far over to the right he cannot sit back up on his own.

---

[16] Artherial scoliosis – Hardening of veins

Made funny faces at his granddaughter. Tried to ask a question but couldn't get the words out.

Thursday – Mom remains in ICU. There is a huge bandage around her skull to protect the brain where the bone has been removed. The nurses continue daily treatment of changing the bed sheets and rubbing lotion on Mom's back. I got my hands on was a Nora Roberts novel to read to Mom. It was excellent hospital material as it wasn't anything too serious. It also wasn't too embarrassing, so it was an excellent choice for Mom and me.

So, I read when visiting Mom. It was interesting walking into Mom's room and her brother, Uncle Scott was reading the book to her. I think I was walking when Uncle Scott was reading about her hair being long and silky and some guy caressing it. It was a little freaky for me! But it did pass the time and I do think that Mom could hear and it was nice being able to sit with her and hopefully give her some smiles on the inside. I would watch her face sometimes for any reaction and even though I saw none, I felt that inside she enjoyed listening to us read to her.

I recall Mom telling me her favorite book was "*King of the Wind.*" I found the book at a store in town and began to read it to Mom. I remember crying the entire time. I hoped that possibly Mom could hear me read and she would know that we cared for her so very much and we were hoping for a recovery.

Thursday evening – Dad wakes up at dinnertime. He says no at first then Uncle Scott and I put the food in front of him. When Dad gets his bearings, I told him what the food was. Dad grabs the fork with his left hand and feeds himself. Dad eats just about all of the mashed potatoes, chicken, peaches and chocolate pudding. Dad asks again why he is in the hospital. I explain he had a stroke and it affected the right side. He was here to make the right side work again. I told him he wouldn't be here long that he would be going to Concord. He tried to ask me another question but couldn't get it out and his eyes teared up. I told him to just take it slow that it would come to him. '

The nurse comes in to tell us it's 7:00 and we needed to leave.

Jennifer Truman * 9132 victor!

Friday, August 13th

6:00pm (Fri) - My younger sister visited Mom this evening and Lucie the day nurse said that Mom's temperature spiked today, but they took care of it. She mentioned that they will be doing another MRI at 8:30pm tonight.

Approximately 8:00pm (Fri) – I visited read more of *"King of the Wind."*

Approximately 8:30pm – The night nurse took Mom in for an MRI and told me we'll know the results tomorrow.

Saturday, August 14th

Approximately 9:00am – Dr. Collis did rounds and saw Mom. He said her temperature went up to 102 degrees yesterday and that they would check the antibiotics and adjust them if need be.

When we questioned him about the latest MRI for Mom, he explained that he did not see a change but that Dr. Simmons' staff would find us and tell us the results of the MRI. Saw eye twitching and the blood pressure was down to 144/86. They saw two spots of bleeding in the brain with the original one on the brain stem.

Chapter Fourteen

Friday, August 13th in what appeared to be in direct defiance of the superstitious date, Dad was able to take pills by mouth and swallowed them. I was hopeful that this was a good sign. Now that he could swallow, he could be taken off of the IV!

Like most stroke victims, Dad couldn't speak and had difficulty using his right side. Dad was very right side dominant and this would be his source of major frustration. It was encouraging that he recognized our family faces. He could even sort of say his granddaughter's name.

As I watched for other signs of improvement, I was happy to see that he ate a good breakfast and by mid morning, polished off ice cream for a snack. It felt like things were finally coming together again. I spoke with the doctor and he felt that Dad was ready for more aggressive speech and physical therapy. So by 10am, he had clearance to move to HealthSouth in Concord, New Hampshire.

I assured Dad that I would be in Concord waiting for his arrival. I wanted him to have a familiar face in the new environment.

The transportation ambulance got him to Concord and he was in his new room at HealthSouth by 12:30pm. Paula would be helping Dad with Occupational therapy, Matt and Gina would be working with Dad on his speech and Susan completed the therapy by working with physically.

By mid-afternoon, Dad had a snack in front of Gina. We watched as she made mental notes of how he cleaned out all his food from the right side. The rest of the afternoon was spent meeting his various therapists, case managers and nurses. I had made arrangements with the hospital to have an information code setup for Mom and Dad. They were to have no visitors unless we called it in.

We were given a menu of choice for his meals the next day and I would read off the items and Dad would either grimace at me or not. I became pretty good at determining which expressions were a vote of disapproval. Because of Dad's limited right side mobility and feeling, most of his food was mashed up like baby food. I thought Dad was going to spit it up like a baby at first. He shoves the container in my face with a "what's this crap?" look. Thankfully when Dad tasted the pudding, he brightened. Thank goodness for chocolate pudding.

"Dad, I promise, as soon as you can feel more, I will get you more regular food. C'mon, just put up with this for a few more days, okay?" I coaxed. I watched his face and he reluctantly agreed.

His speech therapy and occupation therapy began. Dad could see a picture of a cat, say the letters, but not say "cat." He could meow and say "fur," but the brain couldn't come up with cat. I was told this was very common and it just required retraining of the brain. The physical training for Dad went very well.

Even though Dad tired easily, the therapists were amazed at Dad's strength. So, each day I would try to get to Concord for lunch and either the morning therapy or afternoon therapy. Dad was asleep most of the other times, so there wasn't much reason for me to be there.

I was finally back at my house, sleeping in my bed. By then, I had told some girlfriends about my problem with sleeping and that's when I discovered that most of my friends are on drugs. They all gave me samples of their prescriptions. Not being on any medication, I was leery of taking the full amount, so I broke them in half. I finally found a combination that would allow me to sleep for four hours.

I was able to get an appointment with my nurse practitioner, who, thankfully, didn't scold me for my trial period. What I wanted, she decided was a low enough dosage and she gave me a prescription.

It's amazing how just a few hours of downtime for the brain can help rejuvenate me so much. After a couple of nights, I almost felt human again.

Chapter Fifteen

My days consisted of driving to Concord or Hanover, spending time with one parent then drive to the other hospital and spend time with the other parent. Then I would drive home and console myself by snuggling with my cats. Each day I was spending approximately 4 ½ hours in the car, but it was something I had to do.

On Tuesday the 17th, one of the doctors asked me if my parents had living wills. I honestly didn't know. I thought about what lawyer they would have used to file their will. Later I would recall being at Mom and Dad's seeing an envelope with a Boca Raton address on it lying on the desk in their summer house. I remembered Dad saw my confusion at the address and explained what was in the envelope. "Just in case anything happens, this is my law firm."

But at that moment, my mind was a jumbled mess and couldn't seem to remember anything. I had to call friends of our family, current and previous banks, and found one in Syracuse who luckily did know the correct attorney who had the will for my parents and I was able to contact him and have the documents sent to me.

The doctors at Dartmouth wanted a meeting to discuss Mom. The removal of part of her skull relieved the pressure but Mom wasn't getting any better. The doctors wanted to do another round of MRI's and wanted the family to discuss options. The meeting included the Chief of Neurology, Head of ICU and a doctor from radiology. They looked at their collective scheduling and decided that Wednesday at 2:30pm would work for them. My youngest sister and her daughter had already headed back to Florida, so I told my other sister, aunt and uncle of the meeting.

My sister said it would be more convenient for her if we could schedule for later in the afternoon. I told her that wasn't possible, so my uncle stated he would be there with me. I was relieved not to be the sole representative of the family in such a difficult and important matter.

Wednesday morning I drove to Concord and visited with Dad for his morning therapy. In just five days, Dad's improvements were remarkable. He could form some words and mostly get his questions asked. He finally slowed down his eating and chewed most of the food in his mouth then cleared his mouth with liquid before eating another bite. He harrumphed, but he let me check his mouth to make sure no pieces of food could possibly be lodged in his throat. This was of particular concern if he was eating his evening meal as he could have food lodged in his throat and choke while he was sleeping.

When I asked him to clear his mouth, he would do an exaggerated tongue swish, then run his finger in the perimeters of his mouth. Then, he would look at me with that exasperated "fine?" I'd smile and say yes. After lunch, Dad went to his room for his nap and I drove up to Dartmouth for the meeting.

At 2:30pm, Uncle Scott, the doctors and I meet in a conference room in ICU. One of them started describing the type of stroke Mom suffered. Most strokes common in men are located in the basal area of the temporal lobe, like Dad's. Mom's stroke was more severe and was located in the brain stem. While the brain has protection mechanisms, the brain stem does not. They showed us the MRI pictures and more than ¾ of Mom's brain stem was dark which meant no blood flow, which equated to no life. Furthermore, the pictures of Mom's brain being dark meant that she was brain dead. In fact, the machines she was on were the only things keeping her alive.

I handed the doctors Mom's living will which I had been able to get. When they read it they said that there was no decision to be made. Mom made it very clear she did not want artificial life support. .

As the doctor read over the living will again, I felt he was searching for words rather than re-reading the document. He finally put the papers down and looked at me.

"Miss Truman, as we explained to you and your uncle a few moments ago, your mother is brain dead. After reading the living will and considering her physical state, I am recommending that we take your Mom off life support immediately." he said as delicately as he could.

"No," I responded quickly. "There is family that needs to come in and I want Dad to be here to say his goodbyes." I quietly explained. The situation suddenly felt so surreal. Logically, I know Dad probably wouldn't have known what was going on, but I felt that this was important. The doctors knew of our situation and agreed to a few extra days until I could gather everyone together.

Our meeting concluded and the doctors went on with their busy day. When I got to the waiting area of ICU, my sister had just arrived.

"The meeting just finished…" I began as I was about to let her know what was decided.

"What do you mean the meeting just finished?" she angrily interrupted. "I called the hospital and told them to delay the meeting until I got here!"

I was surprised at her announcement especially when I found out later that she and her husband had company at their home and she didn't feel that it was proper etiquette to leave before the guests. There was nothing I could do. The decisions were made according to Mom and Dad's wishes and that was that. I had other issues I needed to address.

Now I had to work on getting Dad transferred back to Dartmouth to see his wife one last time but not really understand the grave circumstances. On Thursday at HealthSouth in Concord, I discussed with the director about our situation. She said it would be no problem as they could plan a day trip. By lunch, everything was set for Dad to be transported the next day to Dartmouth Hitchcock to see Mom.

I called cousins in Arizona and they booked a flight for Saturday. Meanwhile, Thursday evening I got a call from the hospital. Dad's fever spiked and he was transferred next door to the Concord Hospital. I was assured that this was just a precautionary measure and that he'd be fine.

Friday morning I drove to Concord to see Dad. He was still running a fever, but it had come down a bit. Leg pressurizers were on his legs to keep from clotting and he looked exhausted. The day trip to Dartmouth was out of the question.

I spoke with the director of HealthSouth to see what we could do, and she said that I could request a transfer although Concord Hospital may not like this. I called Dartmouth Hitchcock and spoke with our social worker there. She agreed that was the best course of action and began the necessary steps up there. I met with the director at Concord and explained the situation. Judging from the look on his face, he was clearly displeased that I wanted to transfer Dad.

"Look, it has absolutely nothing to do with the level of care my Dad received from your hospital," I began. "The only reason I am requesting this is because I feel that Dad should see his wife before she's taken off life support. This is a social sympathy transfer and nothing else." I was looking him directly in the eye and being as honest and as truthful as I could be. There was a moment I think, when I said that I felt Dad should see his wife before she is taken off life support that I was able to see his disapproval sway. He sat for a moment and then signed the necessary papers and pushed them toward me. I could tell from that simple gesture that he saw the situation as it really was.

Now that I had the paperwork, it had to be sent to Dartmouth Hitchcock where Dad would get entered into the system. When a bed opened up, we would get a call. By the end of the day, I was exhausted and didn't make it to Dartmouth to see Mom. It was the only day I missed and something I felt bad about. When I got back to my home, I went to a friend's birthday party. I guess I needed to see the complete circle of life instead of just one side.

Chapter Sixteen

In the midst of coordinating hospitals and getting paperwork together for a transfer for my Dad, one of my cousins was getting married in Vermont on Saturday the 21st. My sister from Florida had flown in with her daughter and was staying with me at my house

On Saturday, we got the call that there would be a bed available for Dad that afternoon. Between my two sisters and me, it was decided that I would help Dad with the transfer and they would go to the wedding in Stowe, Vermont. I went down to Concord and sat with Dad who was awake. The doctor came in and asked if Dad was ready. When he looked questioningly at the doctor, I spoke up, "I haven't told him yet." The doctor nodded and excused himself out of the room.

I could feel tears beginning to well up in my eyes and wanted to explain the situation without too many tears.

"Dad, we're going back to Dartmouth to go see Mom," I began watching him for a reaction trying to search for the right words.

"Mom isn't doing too well and we need to go see her. Do you understand?" I asked. Dad looked at me and his eyes began filling with tears but he didn't say anything. Then a split moment later, just like that, the thought was forgotten. About an hour later, the ambulance was there to drive Dad back to Dartmouth. I gave him a kiss and told him I would see him at the other end of his ride.

About an hour and a half later, I met Dad at Dartmouth. He was settled into a room which had a television so I turned it on and found a football game. Dad and I watched the game for awhile and I told him I would be checking on Mom. At this point it was about 9pm. I went up to ICU and told Mom that Dad was in the building to come see her. I took out the book I was currently reading and read to Mom.

About an hour later, I finished up the chapter and was putting the book away when one of the nurses came over and said that the first floor was calling me. I went to the phone and they said they needed me downstairs right away. I ran and when I got to Dad's room there was at least 12 people working on him. My heart stopped beating and I felt like I was going to faint. A nurse sat me in a chair and explained what happened.

While I was upstairs, a nurse came around for a routine check and Dad pointed to his chest indicating he had pain. They took him for a scan and while in the elevator, a team from DART (the Dartmouth Hitchcock helicopter medical team) noticed Dad did not look well. He was whisked back into his room where tubes were shoved down his throat and IV's hooked up. I arrived to see the end of this flurry of activity . They began to wheel him out and I stroked Dad's forehead and tried to reassure him.

"Everything will be okay, don't worry, Dad."

"It will be if you get out of the way!" one of the doctors barked at me. So I moved out of the way and Dad was wheeled up to the third floor, ICU, the same ICU where Mom laid.

I tried to call my sisters on the cell but at the Snowflake Inn, but there is no cell phone service. I got the front office and asked for my sisters. I told them the situation and I told them what I knew up to this point. They said they'd drive over in the morning.

About thirty minutes passed before the ICU waiting room phone rings. I answer and I am asked to come back to ICU. I meet two people in the hall and they bring me into a room where they explain that Dad has had a pulmonary embolism and did not survive.

As the reality of this sunk in, I couldn't speak. I can't begin to explain the wave of shock and disbelief that washed over me at that instant. I think I tried to crawl up the wall to get away from the words. I asked to see Dad and they said they would let me know when I could come in. I went back into the waiting room and tried to call the Snowflake Inn. No one answered the phone. I called my cousins from Arizona. They had landed in Manchester, NH and had settled into their room 10 minutes prior to my call. They immediately packed up and drove north. The hotel was kind enough not to charge them for the night.

I called my neighbor and friend Darlene and woke her up. I was babbling how I couldn't get hold of my sisters and didn't know what to do. She suggested calling the police department to ask them to go over to the Inn. Darlene offered to come up and I told her my cousins were on their way. She was relieved that I wouldn't be alone for long.

I called the Police Department in Stowe, Vermont and made my request to send someone over when I was asked what to say. I thought for a moment and in my numbed state, I simply said, "Tell them their Dad had died, thank you." The officer was silent for a moment and asked if I really wanted him to say that and I said yes. There wasn't a delicate way to say it. And, if there was, I was in no condition to think of one. I didn't want my sisters thinking they couldn't call until morning to reach me. I knew I wouldn't be sleeping.

From what I was told, the officer went over to the Inn and walked in where the wedding reception was going on. A cousin saw the officer and had an "uh-oh" feeling. He went to the officer who said he was looking for my sisters. My cousin led the officer to my sister's rooms where the officer had to give them the bad news.

Chapter Seventeen

Meanwhile, I was allowed into Dad's ICU room. Dad was already cold to the touch and his skin had no life. The room had been cleaned up and sterilized and the mess they must have made earlier had been totally removed. There was my Dad…Dead.

Here was the man who was larger than life for me. I looked up to him as a kid, someone I challenged as a teenager and someone I came to dearly love as an adult. And now, he is laying stiff and cold in front of me on August 21, 2004. It's not something you think you will ever have to see and when you do, it is heart wrenching

The nurses told me I had a call and could pick it up in Dad's room. I picked it up and it was my sisters. I told them what happened since my last call. At first they were going to come over in the morning but ended up driving over right away.

At this time, we decided that it was time to let Mom go and I told the nurses she should be taken off life support.

The life support for Mom had been removed pretty quickly, actually done before my sisters arrived. I sat with Mom and explained what happened to Dad. I told her it was okay to go on because Dad was there waiting for her.

The nurses informed me my sisters had arrived and were in the waiting room and on their way back into the ICU. I met them in the hallway and in the only one moment on record, there wasn't any animosity among the three sisters. We had a group hug. We went back to see Dad. My cousins arrived and we all said our last goodbyes to Dad and then the hospital staff came and took Dad away.

We were allowed to stay with Mom all night. My younger sister and I slept on the floor with pillows we grabbed from the waiting room. My cousin encouraged me to eat around lunchtime and I managed some food. My sister requested a minister in Mom's ICU room. We had a small service of me and my sisters, my cousins, uncle and aunt.

That evening, approximately 23 hours after Dad's death, my Mom took her last breath on August 22, 2004.

~~~

Jennifer Truman * 9132 victor!

Sent: *Tuesday, August 24, 2004 5:55 AM*

Subject: *From Jennifer Truman*

It is with a broken heart that I tell you of the passing of both Mom and Dad, Dani and Bill. As you know, August 9th, both Mom and Dad had a stroke. Both were flown to Dartmouth Hitchcock Hospital. Dad was doing great and had been moved to the Rehab hospital. Mom was still at Dartmouth in ICU in a coma. Last week, Dad got a bladder infection, then started spiking temps of 104. He was admitted to Concord Hospital.

On Saturday we, the daughters, requested Dad to be transferred to Dartmouth so he could see Mom one last time. I spent the day with Dad in Concord and met him at Dartmouth when he was moved Saturday evening about 7. Dad was settled in and I went and spent some time with Mom. A nurse came to me about 9:30 and said I was requested downstairs. I went to Dad's room to find a team of doctors working on him. He had a seizure. He was intubated and then transferred to the ICU, the same place Mom was. I waited outside and called my sisters to let them know.

At 10:30 the doctors came to tell me that Dad had a large blood clot move into his lung and he did not make it. After talking to my sisters, we decided it was time to let Mom go. She never came out of her coma and the doctors felt she never would. We abided by her Living Will.

23 hours after Dad, Mom passed away. By her side were her three daughters, her brother and sister-in-law, three nephews and two nieces. We can only believe that Dad wanted to be there to greet Mom on the other side. 23 is also the family number and they were together Aug 23rd for their 41st wedding anniversary. I believe that Mom and Dad are soul mates and neither would have been happy here without the other.

A service will be held for both Mom and Dad, together. Calling hours will be Friday, August 27th from 6-9pm at Wilkinson-Beane Funeral Home, 164 Pleasant St. Laconia, NH

The service will be Saturday, August 28 at 11am at the Congregational Church of Laconia, 18 Veterans Sq. Laconia

A lunch will follow at a place not yet determined.

It has been a difficult two weeks, but knowing you are there has been a comfort to my sisters and me. We will miss two incredible wonderful people, but knowing they are together, forever can only make us feel that this was meant to be.

Jennifer Truman * 9132 victor!

Hugs and kisses,

Jennifer

Epilogue

I t took me two years to "wake up" from my state of shock. Not a day goes by that I don't think of Mom & Dad. I can only hope that they are somewhere off together traveling the world or more. I am blessed that these two people were my parents. They gave me the strength, courage, and wisdom to go on with life.

Frequently, friends of Mom and Dad tell me how much they are missed even after a few years have gone by. My biggest fear was that they would be forgotten, but I know that they touched so many lives in a wonderful way, they'll always be remembered.

When people learn of my story, the question I most often get is "How're you doing?" Well, I am doing better than I was August 9, 2004. I am doing better than I was last year. I am doing better than I was last month and I'm even doing better than I was yesterday. I don't believe in the adage "time heals *all wounds." We chose to either continue on with life or don't, but the wounds are still there.*

I was encouraged to see a therapist after this ordeal. A prior experience after my divorce made me skeptical. The first thing that therapist wanted was to put me on drugs. I disagreed. I was getting divorced; I was supposed to be upset. I didn't think it should be masked by drugs. But, I decided I would give it another try. I went to the therapist, but I didn't know what it was I needed from him. I would have to say he didn't know how to help me either. That ended after a few sessions.

It was that next summer I visited the club where my parents were members. One of their friends came up to me and said they had just been thinking of my folks and how much they were missed. I realized that what I was looking for and needed, I already had. I didn't want Mom and Dad to be forgotten. I am constantly reassured that they have not been forgotten.

Just last week I got some mail from my mom's childhood best friend. She was rearranging some keepsakes and came across a birthday card Mom had sent her. After rereading it, she thought I should have it. "Dear M.L. – I bought this just after we returned to Fla on the 30th – where on earth do the days go? Hope your birthday was a happy one.

We were in New Hampshire for Christmas and it's been so long since I've driven on icy roads, I was terrified to venture out on the roads by myself. Also, the only vehicle we have up there in the winter is a pickup truck which I'm not too fond of driving. None of that bothers Jennifer – she zips all over the place but then, at almost 17, she isn't intimidated by much of anything.

Just re-reading this has nearly blinded me. It's not terribly good stationery. Hope your eyes are still working. Write and let me know how you are. Hope 1984 brings good health and much happiness. Love, Dani"

Getting this old birthday card in the mail more than four years after Mom's death is a sweet reminder of that, indeed, Mom and Dad have not been forgotten.

So, as each day gets a little better, I will eventually figure out what I want to do. I do know that I will not be getting my pilot's license. I have been in small planes since the ordeal and I am fine. I just don't want to be the pilot.

I do know I will continue to play golf. I worked at getting my handicap down to a 10 which is pretty darn good for a girl. I hope that I can maintain my 10 handicap or possibly get even better. I have found a few coaches who I enjoy learning from and try to pass on my knowledge to women who are learning to play golf at no charge.

I know that I will always be an amateur and that allows me to enjoy being on the golf course. It bothers me when people get so upset over this game of golf. We are amateurs; it will not be our source of income. Why get so upset?

My golf has allowed me to stay in touch with some of the men in my Dad's golf circle. Dad had formed his Wednesday golf group both in New Hampshire and Florida. He told me that it was his way of controlling who got to play. You didn't have to be a great golfer but you did have to have a great sense of humor. When I'm visiting the club in Florida, I get to have lunch with the boys. It thrills me that the golf group is still going strong.

I do know I will continue to travel. Mom and Dad gave me the love of travel and I love seeing different places and learning about different cultures. After I lost my parents, I went on a cruise in New Zealand for Christmas. I had a great two weeks. It hurt to sit at Christmas dinner knowing I would never sit with my parents again. I hurt to have the year turn from 2004 to 2005. I sat alone on one of the deck chairs and cried.

Between, I got to see wonderful towns and farms on both the North and the South islands. A group of us rode the jet boats on the Shot Over River, a must for anyone in the area. I also decided that I had to bungee jump off the K-bridge which is short for Kawarau Bridge, another must for anyone in Queenstown.

For those who have not bungee jumped, it is an experience of a lifetime. You start by walking out an old car bridge. Some of the wood planks are gone and you have to walk out to the middle of the bridge. There are two ropes to choose from. One for if you don't want to get wet, the other if you want to take a dunk in the cold river. I choose to stay dry.

I watched a few people do the bungee jumping then decided I better do it before I chicken out. I get in line and a very muscular guy says something to me. I can't understand him. I turn to the guy behind me and ask if he knew what was just said. He replied he was from Australia and couldn't understand him either. That made me laugh. Apparently, the guy wanted me to sit down on the edge so they could wrap my feet. A towel goes around your calves and ankles then they wrap the rope around and between your calves. The guys help you stand up and you are instructed to hop out to the end of the plank. Yeah right. So, you hop out the gang plank. Out in the distance there's a car bridge. If you want more bounce, you jump towards it, if not you point your hands down towards the water. I did something in between.

When you jump you have some forward motion. Then there is a split moment when the forward motion stops and you keep like you're hanging in the air. It is such a minuscule

amount of time but plenty to think "what the fuck did I just do?"
The next thing you know you are looking at the river. Your
brain catches up and you think, okay, okay, not too bad, there's
the river and I'm heading towards it. Then you hit "the bounce"
and you are going away from the water. Not natural, not
natural. Back towards the water and you are ready to be done.

The small raft which is tethered to shore comes under
you. The guys tell you to tuck your head and do a forward roll
and just lay there. They unwrap the rope and the guys above
hoist it back up to the bridge. The guys in the boat pull the raft
back to shore; you hop out and get to climb back up to the
bridge and building. I do have photographic and DVD evidence
of my jump because most of my friends can't believe I did it.

After I gathered my souvenirs, I realized the bus back
into town would not get me back in time for the dinner cruise. I
hitched a ride with a family who were vacationing in New
Zealand for a month. As we were chatting on the way back to
town, we discovered they lived within a half mile of my cousins
in Tucson, AZ. It amazed me that had been that close in
proximity to each other in Arizona, but never met and now we

were all the way in New Zealand and in the same car. Small world.

In July, I went to Kenya and Tanzania. They are two countries my parents had visited in the past. This was a phenomenal trip. I got to see many lions, lioness, elephants, giraffes, zebras and wildebeest. I got to see three leopards and my favorite, the cheetah. During the trip, we rode on two balloon rides. One was in Kenya over the Maasai Mara and the other was in Tanzania over the Serengeti.

We are up at four in the morning to get to the balloon liftoff sight. It's cold, it's dark and there's no coffee. We wait to be told we can get into the basket which means crawling in sideways. Sounds strange? The basket is lying on its side. It is almost like laying on your bed with your knees pulled up to your chin, unless you are on the bottom. Then flip you mattress and hang on. The balloon heats and rises into the air which lifts the basket off the ground and you are finally upright.

As we float above the ground, we get to see the magnificent sunrise. On both balloon rides, just after the sunrise, I released some of Mom and Dad's ashes. I thought it would be nice for them to always be where they could enjoy watching the animals of Africa.

Most of their ashes were scattered at sea in the British Virgin Islands. Mom's mom passed away and she, her brother and the spouses did a sail boat cruise in the British Virgin Islands. They got to a spot and dropped anchor. Mom felt it was the right spot to spread her mom's ashes. While they were spreading ashes at sunset, dolphins jumped out of the water. Mom came back home and informed me that was the spot she wanted her ashes. Thankfully, I remembered this.

One year after Mom and Dad passed away; we chartered a boat out of Tortola and went to the same spot Mom mentioned. We didn't get dolphins jumping out of the water but we did have an interesting school of feeding fish swim by. It was decided that the ashes of Dad would also be spread along with Mom's. Dad had not said he wanted his ashes to go anywhere in particular, so we decided that he gets to travel with Mom.

So, I will wander this world, I will play golf and I will figure it out.

Enjoy every day as much as you can, you never know which one will be your last.

~~~

LaVergne, TN USA
17 August 2009
155042LV00001B/20/P